PETROLEUM REFINING IN INDIA

Reform and Technical Efficiency in Public Sector Enterprises

Sardar Patel Institute of Economic and Social Research Monograph No. 25

PETROLEUM REFINING IN INDIA

Reform and Technical Efficiency in Public Sector Enterprises

Madhusudan Datta

ALLIED PUBLISHERS PRIVATE LIMITED

New Delhi • Mumbai • Kolkata • Chennai • Nagpur
Ahmedabad • Bangalore • Hyderabad • Lucknow

ALLIED PUBLISHERS PRIVATE LIMITED

1/13-14 Asaf Ali Road, **New Delhi**–110002
Ph.: 011-23239001 • E-mail: delhi.books@alliedpublishers.com

47/9 Prag Narain Road, Near Kalyan Bhawan, **Lucknow**–226001
Ph.: 0522-2209942 • E-mail: lko.books@alliedpublishers.com

17 Chittaranjan Avenue, **Kolkata**–700072
Ph.: 033-22129618 • E-mail: cal.books@alliedpublishers.com

15 J.N. Heredia Marg, Ballard Estate, **Mumbai**–400001
Ph.: 022-42126969 • E-mail: mumbai.books@alliedpublishers.com

60 Shiv Sunder Apartments (Ground Floor), Central Bazar Road,
Bajaj Nagar, **Nagpur**–440010
Ph.: 0712-2234210 • E-mail: ngp.books@alliedpublishers.com

F-1 Sun House (First Floor), C.G. Road, Navrangpura,
Ellisbridge P.O., **Ahmedabad**–380006
Ph.: 079-26465916 • E-mail: ahmbd.books@alliedpublishers.com

751 Anna Salai, **Chennai**–600002
Ph.: 044-28523938 • E-mail: chennai.books@alliedpublishers.com

5th Main Road, Gandhinagar, **Bangalore**–560009
Ph.: 080-22262081 • E-mail: bngl.books@alliedpublishers.com

3-2-844/6 & 7 Kachiguda Station Road, **Hyderabad**–500027
Ph.: 040-24619079 • E-mail: hyd.books@alliedpublishers.com

Website: www.alliedpublishers.com

ISBN : 978-81-8424-679-7

Published by Sunil Sachdev and printed by Ravi Sachdev at Allied Publishers Pvt. Ltd.,
Printing Division, A-104 Mayapuri Phase II, New Delhi -110064

Foreword

It is a matter of great personal satisfaction to me that Prof. Madhusudan Datta has completed an important study on the Technical Efficiency of the Oil Refining Sector in India and published it as a monograph of the Sardar Patel Institute of Economic and Social Research. This has significance for a number of reasons.

The Sardar Patel Institute's Monograph Series in 70's and 80's had a number of important contributions in the field of Industrial Economics. These included structural and policy studies in subjects like industrial complex analysis, inter-regional planning models and important monographs for the small scale sectors which were first ones to explain the dynamism of sectors like diamond polishing and art-silk. Many of these pioneering pieces of work and publications became very popular subsequently. There was then a lull on account of various reasons and it has been broken by this important book. As Chairman of BICP, I was asked to study the pricing mechanism of India's Oil Refining Sector. It was an economist's nightmare. Full cost pricing encouraged the coexistence of oil refineries, where conversion costs were sometimes almost thrice to those of the best. Many well meaning proposals of reforms were side stepped by procedures which were implemented by the operational Ministry. Prof. Datta's study is a definitive piece of work of this epoch and period since then.

Prof. Datta has been very careful in data collection and use, both on the revenue and the cost side. For example non-production costs are excluded. He uses fairly recent production function techniques but finds that the old reliable Cobb Douglas Production Functions with efficiency specified give the best results.

Prof. Datta's work covers a period of eighteen years. He studies the functioning of the public sector enterprises over the period as a whole and also by dividing the period in two parts. The first part concerns the APM regime while the second relates to the working of a market regime with subsidies built in for the oil companies. Of the two periods, he finds only in the post-APM regime evidence of rising efficiency. This suggests that the improving performance observed for the period as a whole was on account of the performance in the post APM period.

The finding of rising efficiency during the post-APM period remained even after NRL, a company which was not there in the panel for the earlier period, was excluded. Economic reform undertaken in 1991 was not, by itself, of significance to the efficiency of public sector oil refineries but subsequent dismantling of the APM was aimed at enhancing efficiency of refinery operations. Dr. Datta presents strong evidence of this aim being realized. This is more so since Prof. Datta's work does not take into account product quality changes. Accounting for that would accentuate the results. Emphasis on product quality as well as maintenance of environmental norms has gradually gathered momentum and they have been strong particularly during the more recent period. While this generally meant use of more factor inputs per barrel of crude his measure of product does not account for quality improvement. This means, as the author rightly argues, efficiency improvements captured by his models are underestimates of the actual performance.

I am very happy that the study is being published as the Sardar Patel Institute's monograph and the credit for restarting the monograph series goes to former Director Prof. Niresh Shah, who has recently superannuated.

I congratulate both Prof. Datta and Prof. Shah for this achievement.

Yoginder K. Alagh
Professor Emeritus, SPIESR

March 11, 2011

Preface

The present work started as an ICSSR project. The basic result of the study was published in the Journal of Quantitative Economics in 2008. As the result was very interesting and it stood on a rather small data base I was keen on verifying it with an extended database. As fresh data became available I felt the twitch but burden of other works and lethargy were preventing a fresh venture. At this time inspiration came form Professor Y.K. Alagh who encouraged bringing out monograph of the SPIESR and he has been kind enough to write a Foreword for the monograph.

Some of the chapters of the book bear some resemblance to the corresponding chapters of the ICSSR project report. But except Chapter 1, all the other chapters are either thoroughly-revised-and-extended versions of the report or entirely new. Chapter 4 is new and results presented in Chapter 7 are new as they cover four additional years generating twenty-four new observations. At the end of the venture it gives me satisfaction that the new results strengthen the conclusion of the earlier study.

For performance evaluation of the public sector oil-refining units I realized that it would be ideal to have data at the plant level. These data are available from published sources only in isolated fragments. The ICSSR project gave me the opportunity to visit some refineries. It was only after a few visits that I realized how closely guarded the data are and even these data are not organized in a way that would reveal the required information for me. After much effort I gave up the hope of generating data series at the plant level and decided to concentrate on published data at the company level. The major sources of published data are the Public Enterprises Survey of the Department of Public Enterprises, Ministry of Heavy Industry and Public Enterprises, and Indian Petroleum and Natural Gas Statistics published by the Ministry of Petroleum and Natural Gas, of the Government of India. The two sources are very rich with information about the petroleum scenario but they do not provide plant level data relevant for an analysis of efficiency.

I visited four refineries of four different companies—NRL, BPCL (Mahul), HPCL (Trombay) and IOCL (Haldia). Though I could not collect time series data on factors of production, the visits, nevertheless, were extremely useful. I met a good number of high level functionaries, including GMs, DGMs and high level technicians, in these companies. I tried to understand the problems and the challenges. These visits helped me to form an understanding about the nature of machinery and equipments at work and the nature of their depreciation and maintenance. All these experiences gave me some confidence to talk about the subject.

But the problem about obtaining the right type of data, even at the company level, still remained. I realized that the greatest challenge in the measurement of factors of production came from capital input. When we have the book values, and the question is how to transform the book values of fixed capital stock (gross block) into estimates of real fixed capital stock. The Perpetual Inventory Method (PIM) gives a way out and it is widely used by researchers. After analyzing the method I came to understand that PIM gives the wealth stock, not the productive capacity of the stock. The OECD and the BLS are working in this area. For a proper analysis of efficiency we needed an index of capital service. In fact, I was seized with this conceptual problem even before the ICSSR project started. Fortunately, it seems, I could come up with some sort of a solution and did not have to make a compromise by opting for the use of the inappropriate wealth stock in our analysis. In this regard discussions with Paul Shreyer of the OECD, Paris, were helpful. Thus the principal challenge in the work was how to get the right kind of data. Once refined data were ready, the rest was rather simple. There exist established framework and statistical package for efficiency study. The researcher has to put the data into the econometric programme, get the result and interpret it carefully.

I take this opportunity to express my appreciation to the ICSSR for giving me financial assistance, while I was in Kalyani University, to work on the challenging project and to the SPIESR for encouraging me to extend and update the earlier work to bring out the monograph. In spite of all that my task would have been unbearably difficult without help from a good number of persons of whom S. Dasgupta of NRL deserves special mention. A good number of other people helped me in the refineries. I name below only the most prominent of these knowledgeable friends: A.K. Bhattacharya and R. Hazarika, both from the NRL; S. Chandramohan, M. Venugopal and K. Ravi from the BPCL; R. Ganeshan and R. Sankaran from the HPCL; and C.A. Sudarsanam, A. Ghosh and D. Roy from the IOCL. I must also mention M. Bezbarua for his help.

Pradipta Bhattachary and Mainak Roy helped me in various ways in spite of their very busy schedules. Chapter 2 draws discernibly on Pradipta's Ph.D. thesis done under my supervision. Also, my erstwhile colleague, M. Majumdar, was kind enough to spend a considerable amount of his time trying to give me some lessons in elementary organic chemistry. Three of my students, D. Sil, A. Bhattacharya and M. Bhnuiya helped in data processing.

N.C. Shah, the former director of the SPIESR, helped in various ways and the staff of the institute have been exemplary with their cooperation. Also, it has been a pleasure working with Allied Publishers Private Limited.

And, I had the vital support from my family.

SPIESR, Ahmedabad, **Madhusudan Dutta**
April 4, 2011

CONTENTS

Foreword .... *v*
Preface .... *vii*

1. **Refining Petroleum Crude: A Technical Note** 1
   1.1: Properties of Hydrocarbons 2
   1.2: Composition and Structure of the Components of Petroleum 4
   1.3: Refining the Crude 7

2. **Evolution of Petroleum Refining in India** 9
   2.1: Nascent Petroleum Sector of India 9
   2.2: Maturing Industry and Inadequacy of the Public Sector 12
   2.3: A Broader Perspective 16

3. **Industry Structure and Pricing of Products** 19
   3.1: The Major Players: Upstream Sector 19
   3.2: The Major Players: Downstream Sector 20
   3.3: Price Determination 22

4. **Technical Efficiency and its Measurement** 26
   4.1: The Concept of Efficiency in Production 26
   4.2: Necessary Abstraction of the Reality 29
   4.3: Total Factor Productivity and Technical Efficiency 36
   4.4: Data Generation 38
   4.5: Some Final Comments 40

5. **Estimation of Technical Efficiency Using Stochastic Frontier** 42
   5.1: Production Frontier Models 44
   5.2: Stochastic Production Frontiers 47
   5.3: Maximum Likelihood Estimation: The Normal-Truncated Normal Model 49
   5.4: Some Empirical Applications for the Indian Economy 53

6. **Measurement of Variables** 57
6.1: Capital 57
6.2: Implications of Two Approaches: PIM and OHSM 60
6.3: EPD under the PIM 63
6.4: Measurement of Service Capital 65
6.5: Segregation of Refining and Marketing Operations 70

7. **Technical Efficiency in Oil Refining Public Sector Companies** 77
7.1: Earlier Studies on Performance of Oil Refining PSCs 79
7.2: Production and Inputs 82
7.3: Factor Employment in Refining Operations and Partial Productivities 86
7.4: Technical Efficiency in Oil Refining PSCs 89
7.5: Conclusion 97

References 101

LIST OF TABLES

	Topic	Pages No.
1.1	Products Made by the US Petroleum Industry	3
1.2	Boiling Range in Relation to Number of Carbon Atoms in Hydrocarbons	4
2.1	Indian Refineries as on October 1, 2009	13
2.2	Planned Capacity Expansion During XIth Five Year Plan	14
2.3	Grassroots Refineries Coming Up During XIth Five Year Plan	15
2.4	Petroleum: Production and Self-reliance	17
3.1	Retail Prices of Selected Petroleum Products in Delhi	23
6.1	EPD'S for Service Capital Estimation (d) for Alternative Values of 'r', 'T', and Terminal Efficiency of Capital Goods.	68
6.2	Estimates of Service Capital Indices of PSCs	69
6.3	Fixed Assets of BPCL, 2002-03	71
6.4	Segregation of Fixed Assets According to Purposes	72
A 6.1	Refinery Output of PSCs	74
A 6.2	Refinery Labour Index for PSCs	76
A6.3	Refinery Service Capital Index for PSCs	76
7.1	ML Estimates of Production Function and Technical Efficiency Coefficients	94
7.2	ML Estimates of Production Function and Technical Efficiency Coefficients	96
7.3	Generalized Log-Likelihood Ratio Test of Significance of the Trans-Log Model	97
A7.1	Capital Productivity in Public Sector Refineries	99
A7.2	Labour Productivity in Public Sector Refineries	100
A7.3	Capital Intensity in Public Sector Refineries	100

LIST OF FIGURES

	Topic	Pages No.
2.1	Quinquennial Crude Throughput in Indian Refineries	18
2.2	Sensitive Products in Total Production of PSEs: 2008-09	18
3.1	Retail Prices of Selected Petroleum Products in Delhi	24
4.1	Technical Efficiency with Non-stochastic Frontier	31
4.2	Technical Efficiency with Stochastic Frontier	34
7.1	Capital Productivity	89
7.2	Labour Productivity	90

Chapter 1

Refining Petroleum Crude: A Technical Note

Based on Cassini spacecraft probe scientists announced definitive evidence of existence of lakes and seas filled with liquid methane on Saturn's moon Titan.

Stofan, E.R., *et al.* (2007)

Introduction

Petroleum crude is an inflammable liquid consisting basically of a large and complex variety of hydrocarbons which are organic compounds of hydrogen and carbon bonding in all possible ways. It is found in geological formations and recovered mostly by drilling through the earth's surface. The term petroleum literally means rock oil—petra means rock in Greek and oleum means oil in Latin. Naturally occurring crude oil contains, apart from hydrocarbons, small quantities of organic compounds having nitrogen, oxygen and sulphur and also trace elements of some metals. The molecular composition varies from one geological formation to another. Each petroleum variety has a unique mix of molecules determining the physical and chemical properties like colour (usually black or dark brown) and viscosity. This wonderful substance accounts for a large part of energy consumption in every part of the world – estimated to vary from about one-third of the total in Europe and Asia to more than half of the total in the Middle East.[1] While the lion's share of crude oil is used to meet the energy needs of transportation and for heating and generation of electricity throughout the world, about one-sixth of it is utilized to make a wide range of chemicals like fertilizers and pesticides, pharmaceuticals and plastics.

The hydrocarbon compounds of petroleum are principally molecules of paraffins (alkanes), naphthenes (cycloparaffins), aromatics or combinations of these. Another type of hydrocarbon in refineries' products is olefin (alkene), which is supposed to be generated by decomposition during the

[1] *Source*: U.S. Energy Information Administration 2004, pp.7-14.

distillation of the crude. Principal among other elements (other than carbon and hydrogen) that appear in crude oils are sulphur in the form of free (elemental) sulphur, hydrogen sulphide (H_2S), mercaptan (RSH), thiophene, etc. Sulphur is troublesome in petroleum products as it causes corrosion and produces sulphur dioxide (SO_2) (which is toxic and is the main component of acid rain) when burned. H_2S is a poison. The petroleum industry is a large producer of sulphur recovered from crude and obtained by converting H_2S into elemental sulphur. Nitrogen, arsenic, vanadium, nickel and even oxygen found in different compounds are also problematic. Salt in different forms is another problematic material. It occurs in crude in the form of fine droplets of brine or minute particles of salt. It causes corrosion and depositing in equipments and the corrosion becomes more vicious in combination with H_2S and water.

1.1 Properties of Hydrocarbons

The many hydrocarbons in crude oil vary widely in physical and chemical properties. It is these differences that determine the way in which they are processed in refineries and the way in which the finished products are employed. Early refineries produced their finished products directly from crude oil by distillation alone. Naturally, early processes were rather rudimentary; petroleum-distilled kerosene used in oil lamps often caused explosions until it was realized that some lower-boiling material would need to be removed for safety. Thus improvements took place with experience. With the advent of automobiles and their increasing numbers gradually gasoline became the major product produced by refiners; and gasoline is produced in about 40 different specifications today. Except for some residual fuel oil the products of early refineries were quite different from those produced in today's very complex refineries. With strict environmental regulations in effect and crude's higher sulphur content (as the better crude gets depleted faster), products from crude distillation today require further processing to produce acceptable finished products. While the common man sees only some broad categories of petroleum products such as gasoline, jet fuel, home heating oil, diesel, kerosene etc., a survey of the petroleum refineries and petrochemical plants conducted by the American Petroleum Institute revealed over 2300 products made to individual specifications (given in Table 1.1).

Basically the refinery processes are based on large quantity products such as gasoline, diesel, jet fuel, etc. Storage and waste disposal are expensive and it is necessary to sell or use all the items produced from crude oil; even some materials such as high sulphur heavy fuel oil and fuel grade coke must be sold at less than the cost of crude. As mentioned above the hydrocarbon compounds present in crude oil vary widely in physical and chemical properties. There exist close correlation between the number of carbon atoms per molecule of different series of hydrocarbons on the one hand and their boiling points, flash points, auto ignition temperature, etc. Some major petroleum products are listed in Table 1.2 along with their boiling range and number of carbon atoms.

Table 1.1: Products Made by the US Petroleum Industry

Class	*Number*	*Class*	*Number*
Fuel gas	1	Lubricating oils	1156
Liquefied gases	13	White oil	100
Gasolines	40	Rust preventive	65
Gas turbine (jet) fuels	12	Transformer and cable oils	12
Kerosines	5	Greases	271
Middle distillates (diesel and light fuel oils)	27	Waxes	113
		Asphalts	209
Residual fuel oil	16	Cokes	4
Carbon blacks	5	Chemicals, solvents, miscellaneous	300
Total			2347

Source: Gary and Handwerk (2000) p. 6.

The closeness of properties of hydrocarbons with near number of carbon atoms makes possible their separation by distillation and grouping into categories (as in Table 1.1) that are suitable for different types of uses. However, reality is extremely complicated and varied. So requirements vary widely. Apart from that with the advancement of knowledge regarding effects of different hydrocarbons on environment, refinery products are now extremely varied (as indicated above) and are made to very (and increasingly) stringent specifications. A modern refinery, therefore, invariably consists of several units (other than the crude distillation unit) like the vacuum distillation unit, catalytic cracker unit, hydrocracker unit, alkylation unit and so on. Before going further to take a bird's eye-view of the refining process it should be instructive to take a brief excursion into the chemical composition and structure of the components of petroleum.

Table 1.2: Boiling Range in Relation to Number of Carbon Atoms in Hydrocarbons

	Boiling Range (°F)	*No. of C's*
LPG	(–)44–31	3 – 4
Gasoline	31–400	4 – 11
Kerosene/jet fuel	380–520	10 – 15
Diesel fuel	520–650	15 – 20
Atmospheric gas oil	650 – 800	20 – 25
Atmospheric residue	800 +	25 +
Vacuum gas oil	800 – 1000	25 – 50
Vacuum residue	1000 +	50 +
Petroleum Coke	2000 +	200 +

Specialty products like lubes, greases, carbon black, petrochemical feedstocks, etc. are not considered in the table.
Source: Maples, (2000), p. 30.

1.2 Composition and Structure of the Components of Petroleum

The hydrocarbons present in crude petroleum are classified into three general types: paraffins, naphthenes and aromatics. The fourth type is olefins that are generated during processing by the hydrogenation of paraffins and naphthenes.The paraffin series of hydrocarbons is characterized by the simple rule that carbon atoms are connected by a single bond and the other bonds are saturated with hydrogen atoms. The general formula is C_nH_{2n+2}. When the number of carbon atoms in the molecule is greater than three, several hydrocarbons may exist, which have the same number of carbon and hydrogen atoms but different structures. This is because carbon is capable of not only chain formation, but also of forming single or double branched chains, which give rise to isomers that have significantly different properties. The number of possible isomers increases in geometric progression as the number of carbon atoms increases. There are two paraffin isomers of butane, three of pentane, 17 structural isomers of octane and, by the time the number of carbon atoms has increased to 18, there are 60,533 isomers of cetane. Crude oil contains molecules with up to 70 carbon atoms and, so, the number of possible parffinic hydrocarbons is very high. We take below the simple example of two isomers of Butane (having 4-atoms of Carbon):

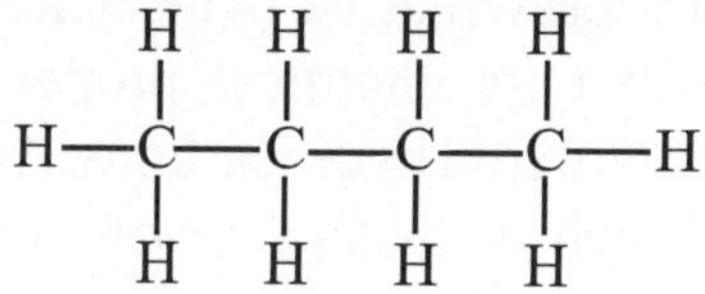

N-Butane

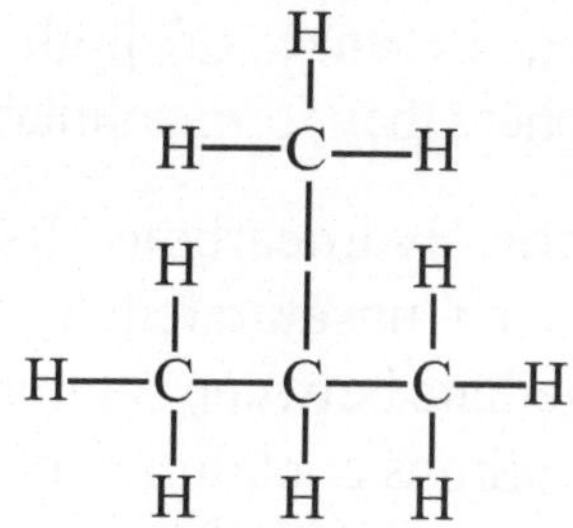

Isobutene

Naphthenes are cycloparaffins in which all the available bonds of carbon atoms are saturated with hydrogen. Cycloparaffins differ in composition from the corresponding paraffins in that they contain two hydrogen atoms less. The general formula is, therefore, C_nH_{2n}. Example:

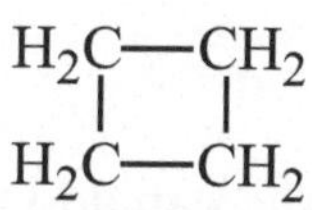

Cyclobutane

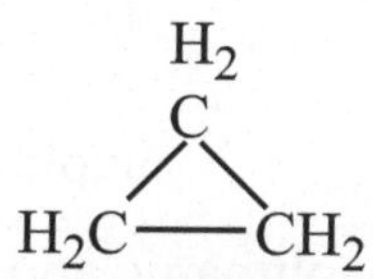

Cyclopropane

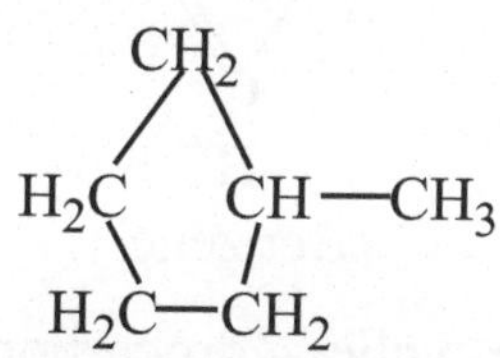

Methylcyclopentane

Cycloparaffins often have lateral chains. The name naphthene comes from Greek naphtha which means rock oil. They have much in common with paraffins—their activity is low and they are combustible. Many types of napthenes are present in crude oil.

Olefins do not occur naturally in crude oil but are formed during their processing. These are unsaturated hydrocarbons. The molecule of each of these unsaturated hydrocarbons has one double bond and therefore each has two hydrogen atoms less than the corresponding saturated hydrocarbon. The composition of these hydrocarbons also is, therefore, expressed by the general formula C_nH_{2n}.[2] Olefins are generally undesirable in finished products because the double bonds are reactive

---

[2] See Organic Chemistry: LA Tsvetkov (1985).

and the compounds are more easily oxidized and polymerized to from gums and varnishes—thus forming filter and equipment plugging. Though some have the desirable property of high research octane number, because of high reaction rates with compounds in the atmosphere they form pollutants and are considered generally undesirable.

Aromatic Hydrocarbons: Its simplest representative is benzene, C_6H_6. This is an unsaturated hydrocarbon but its chemical properties are intermediate between saturated and unsaturated hydrocarbons. Aromatic hydrocarbons contain a benzene ring which is unstable but often behaves as a saturated compound.

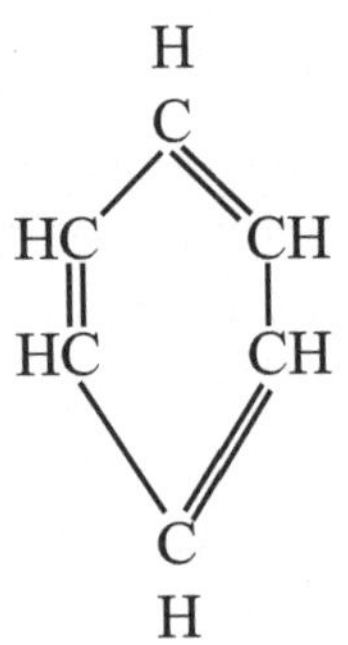

Benzene

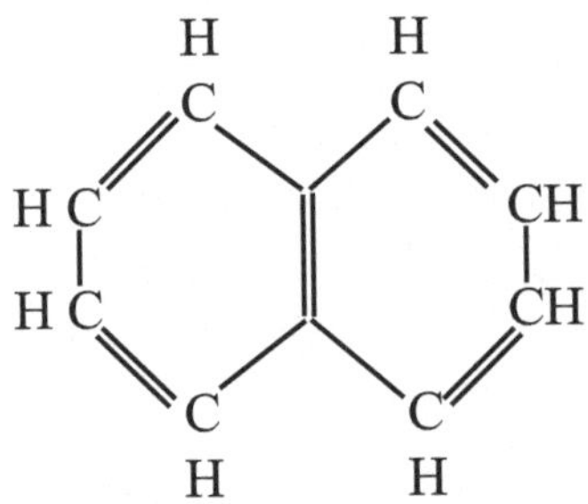

Naphthalene

The cyclic hydrocarbon, both naphthanic and aromatic, can add paraffin side chains in place of some the hydrogen atoms attached to the ring carbons. These mixed types have mixed physical and chemical properties. It is important to note that the different types of hydrocarbons are capable of being transformed into one another under suitable conditions. A modern refinery takes up this whole task keeping in mind the demand for products and the supreme importance of protecting the environment.

Petroleum and Products

As we know, the composition of petroleum varies with locality and petroleum is a mixture of hydrocarbons with a large range of molecular weights and boiling at various temperatures; so it can be distilled into separate fractions. Products of this distillation process are Gasoline (petrol), kerosene, gas oil (diesel), etc. These are referred to as distillates or light petroleum products. A detailed description of the products has already been given in Table 1.1. An important property of petrol is its antiknock property. Paraffins of normal structure are the least stable hydrocarbons with respect to detonation. Branched hydrocarbons and also unsaturated and aromatic hydrocarbons are more stable to detonation. This characteristic is indexed by octane numbers. Straight run gasoline has comparatively low octane number. Improvement of this characteristic requires special method. Obviously, getting so many fractions, and each fraction with so much varied properties, requires extremely sophisticated refining techniques. We discuss the brief outlines below.[3]

1.3 Refining the Crude

The crude oil is heated in furnace and charged to an atmospheric distillation tower. Distillation separates butanes and lighter wet gas (mainly a mixture of pentane, hexane and other light hydrocarbons that are liquid under normal conditions), unstabilized light naphtha, **heavy naphtha**, kerosene, atmospheric gas oil (used as diesel) and topped (reduced) crude (ARC). ARC is a mixture of many hydrocarbons. The topped crude oil is sent to the vacuum distillation tower and separated into vacuum gas oil steam and vacuum reduced crude bottoms (VRC). This is heavy fuel oil or asphalt (if the crude oil is suitable) with a low market value. Decomposition of petroleum hydrocarbons into more volatile substances is known as cracking. There are two types of cracking processes – thermal and catalytic. In thermal cracking high temperature does the job while in the catalytic process the reaction is catalyzed. The VRC from the vacuum tower is thermally cracked in a delayed coker to produce wet gas, coker gasoline, coker gas oil and coke.

The atmospheric and vacuum crude unit gas oils and coker gas oil are used as feedstocks for the catalytic cracking or hydrocraking units. These units crack the heavy molecules into lower molecular weight compounds boiling in the gasoline and distillate fuel ranges. The products from the hydrocracker unit are saturated but the unsaturated catalytic cracker products are saturated and improved by hydrotreating or reforming.

All the light naphtha streams obtained from different units are sent to the isomerization unit to improve their octane numbers by converting straight chain paraffins into isomers. Similarly, heavy naphtha streams

---

[3] We basically follow Maples (2000), and Gary and Handwerk (2001).

are sent to the catalytic reformer for improvements of octane numbers. The products are then blended into regular and premium gasoline.

The middle distillates from the crude, coker and cracking units are blended into diesel, jet fuels and furnace oils. In some refineries (like the Haldia refinery of IOC) the heavy vacuum gas oil and reduced crude from paraffinic or naphthanic base crude oils are produced into lubricating oils.

Each refinery has its own unique processing scheme which is determined by the process equipment available, crude oil characteristics, operating costs and product demand. The optimal flow pattern for any refinery is dictated by economic considerations and no two refineries are identical in their operations.

A modern refinery is the result of evolution over time from a single simple distillation unit to a complex system containing 10 to 15 types of process units. The basic steps of this evolution are as follows (Maples, 2000):

The first advance was from simple batch or differential distillation processes leading to segregation of hydrocarbons according to boiling ranges to continuous distillation. The discovery of thermal cracking made production of higher-octane gasoline possible and so it marked a major advance for the industry. Then the catalytic era began.

As Table 1.2 indicates, the higher-value products (gasoline, jet fuel and diesel) have relatively smaller molecular weights while heavy ends have much higher molecular weights. These heavy ends constitute from 25 to 50 volume percent of crude oil. So, the interest of the refiner is to upgrade these low-value materials to high-value ones by cracking. There are two basic processes: 1. removal of carbon by forming coke and 2. direct addition of hydrogen. The first process is relatively inexpensive. The second process is more difficult and expensive.

Catalytic cracking has endured more than 60 years and remains the conversion workhorse of the refinery by virtue of continual improvement in mechanical design and catalyst development. Catalytic reforming also has a similar distinction. Alkylation and isomarization are also two areas of great importance in terms of built-up capacity. But catalytic hydrocracking offers flexibility in product yields not available in other processes. High cost of this process inhibits its rapid growth.

Chapter 2

Evolution of Petroleum Refining in India

The advent of petroleum-refined kerosene saved some species of great whales from extinction by producing an inexpensive substitute for whale oil, thus eliminating the economic imperatives for open-boat whaling.

Robbins, J.S. (1992)

Introduction

History gives evidence of uses of petroleum, particularly as asphalt, form ancient times. The process of distillation to produce kerosene from petroleum was invented by a polish pharmacist, Ignacy Lucasiewicz, who made kerosene lamps available for surgical operation in a hospital on July 31, 1853. This date is considered by many as marking the beginning of the modern petroleum industry. Though Russia had the early lead in oil exploration, by the mid-twentieth century the US became the leading producer of oil. Subsequently, Saudi Arabia far surpassed the US and Russia caught up with the US. India was an insignificant player in the field, either as a producer or as a consumer, in mid-twentieth century.

2.1 Nascent Petroleum Sector of India

Independent India started with total refinery crude throughput of a meager 0.25 metric million tons per annum (MMTPA) and a single refining unit at Digboi set up in 1901 by Assam Oil Company Limited (a subsidiary of Burmah Oil Company). Enthusiasm to build the nation in a big way following a socialistic pattern led the government to pay attention to the rapidly rising demand for oil that economic development was sure to generate. So, the government created a public sector undertaking named ***Indian Refineries Ltd (IRL)*** which was registered in 1958 under the Companies Act of 1956. Country's first public sector refinery came into existence with design capacity of 0.75 MMPTA on January 1, 1962, at ***Guwahati (Assam)*** under the purview of IRL with technical and financial assistance from the Rumanian government. Then, ***Barauni refinery***, aided by Russian technology and expertise, was commissioned in 1964. In the same year the IRL was merged with the marketing venture of the government of India—the ***Indian Oil Company***, established in 1959—to form a wholly owned government corporation which came to be known as ***Indian Oil Corporation Ltd*** (IOC), with the main objective of coordinating and controlling the refining and distribution operations of these two oil companies effectively. The company's refineries division was initially formed to develop and manage the Guwahati and Barauni refineries. Later, the ***Koyali (Gujarat) refinery*** project started by ONGC was also brought under its control. Koyali refinery, built with the soviet technical and financial aid, went on stream in 1965. In addition, IOC acquired the refinery and distribution operation of Assam Oil Co. Ltd in 1981.

Meanwhile, the first-five-year-plan saw the commissioning of three private sector refineries as well. The ***Burmah Shell Refineries Ltd***, incorporated as a private limited company in 1952, became a public limited company in 1956. The refining unit of the company was located at Mumbai. The ***Standard Vacuum Refining Company*** of India Ltd was also set up as a private limited company in 1952 and it was converted to a public limited company in 1953, to run a refinery at Trombay in Mumbai. This refinery went on stream in 1954.The name of the company was changed to ESSO Standard Refining Company of India Ltd in 1962. Another agreement between the Government of India and Caltex (India) Ltd in February 1955 led to the establishment of the ***Caltex Oil Refining (India) Ltd*** (CORIL). Its refinery was set up at Visakhapatnum, and it started commercial production in 1957. In 1966, the total private sector refinery throughput was about 8.2 MT per annum, which was much more than the cumulative throughput of the three public sector refineries at that time.

Another refinery to come into existence was ***Cochin Refineries Ltd (CRL)***. The company was incorporated as a public limited company and went on stream in 1966. The refinery is located at Ambalamugal in Ernaculum district, Kerala. After Visakhapatnum (CORIL) and Ambalamugal (CRL), the third refinery in south India at Manali (Madras)—***Madras Refineries Ltd (MRL)***—was commissioned in July 1969. This refinery, at that time, was unique in nature in as much as it was the first to perform dual operations of refining crude to a wide range of fuel products and producing lube oil base stock (LOBS) under a single roof. In November 1993, MRL has started operating another small refinery unit of 0.5 MMTPA installed refining capacity at ***Narimanum (Penangudi)*** near Nagaputtinum (TamilNadu).

Haldia refinery was erected at Haldi, West Bentgal, in collaboration with M/s Technip-ENSA of Frañce and M/s Industrial Export of Rumania. The refinery was commissioned in 1975. This refinery, like MRL, was also designed to produce lube oil base stocks along with usual fuel products.

Continued growth in demand for petroleum products led to the establishment of ***Bongaigaon Refinery & Petrochemicals Ltd (BRPL)*** in February 1974, in Bongaigaon district in Assam. It was the first refinery in India, which was integrated with a petrochemical complex comprising of Xylene & Dymethyl Terephthalate (DMT) plants and a Polyester Staple Fiber (PSF) plant. This refinery with initial installed capacity of processing 1.35 MTPA crude, stated commercial production in February 1979.

Simultaneously with setting up of new refineries, the decade of seventies saw the nationalization of three out of four private sector refineries in operation at the time. **Bharat petroleum Corporation Ltd.** (BPCL) came into existence in 1976, when the Burmah Shell Refining & Marketing companies (Mumbai) were taken over by the Government of India. In 1974 government of India acquired the assets of ESSO Standard Refining Company of India and Lube India Ltd to form **Hindustan Petroleum Corporation Ltd** (HPCL). After the take over and merger, it became a fully owned government corporation registered under Indian Companies Act. Caltex, which had also been taken over in 1976 was merged with HPCL in 1978. The undertakings of Kosan Gas Co. Ltd were merged with HPCL in May 1979. In effect, HPCL was formed as a "Schedule B" corporation after merging together four different organizations at different points of time. Thus, HPCL operates two refineries, one at Trombay (Mumbai) and the other at Visakhaputnum. The Trombay unit was subsequently developed and designed as the third (after MRL and IOC-Haldia) lube refinery of the country. The last refinery under private control, Digboi (AOC), was taken over by IOC in 1981. IOC set up yet another refinery at **Mathura** (UttarPradesh), sixth under the control of IOC, which went on stream in 1982. Among other major achievements in capacity creation during the 1980s are substantial augmentation of capacities of the two HPCL refineries in Mumbai and Visakhapatnam. Many other refineries also went through the process of capacity augmentation over the whole period.

Until the end of the decade of the fifties the Indian petroleum industry was controlled by a few Anglo-American companies. The newly independent state wanted to play a significant role in this vital industry. The industrial policy resolution of 1948 and 1956 has clearly documented the government's aspiration and future plans for core industries like petroleum exploration and refining. All future development of petroleum industry was reserved for public sector undertakings. But foreign assistance was a necessity for both infusion of capital and technology. As collaboration with Anglo-American oil majors were ruled out, other alternatives were explored. At that time the government considered the following four options for the development of petroleum industry:

1. Seek assistance from a favourably viewed great power, the Soviet Union,
2. Collaborate with a small country, like Rumania, possessing the technology,
3. Explore the possibility of a government to government co-operation with other small but neutral countries like Austria which had developed sufficient technical expertise in petroleum industry by that time, or,
4. Try and develop the industry the hard way through self-help by employing technicians and bringing necessary machinery from any source available.

The government really explored all the alternatives but mainly went for collaboration with the Soviets. However, as the Soviet influence diminished over the years, the US companies and multilateral funding agencies like the World Bank played increasingly significant roles in this sector.

2.2 Maturing Industry and Inadequacy of the Public Sector

During the 1960s a number of oil and gas fields were discovered by ONGC in Gujrat and Assam. Discovery of offshore oil field in Bombay High in 1974 opened up new possibility for greater self reliance in oil. By virtue of new discoveries by ONGC and OIL, by mid-80s India achieved

Table 2.1: Indian Refineries as on October 1, 2009

Sl.No.	*Name of the Company*	*Location of the Refinery*	*Capacity (MMTPA)**
1.	Indian Oil Corporation Limited (IOCL)	Guwahati	1.00
2.	IOCL	Barauni	6.00
3.	IOCL	Koyali	13.70
4.	IOCL	Haldia	6.00
5.	IOCL	Mathura	8.00
6.	IOCL	Digboi	0.65
7.	IOCL	Panipat	12.00
8.	Hindustan Petroleum Corporation Limited (HPCL)	Mumbai	5.50
9.	HPCL	Visakhapatnam	7.50
10.	Bharat Petroleum Corporation Limited (BPCL)	Mumbai	12.00
11.	Chennai Petroleum Corporation Limited (CPCL)	Manali	9.50
12.	CPCL	Nagapattnam	1.00
13.	BPCL, Kochi Refineries Ltd. (KRL)	Kochi	9.50
14.	Bongaigaon Refinery & Petrochemicals Ltd. (BRPL)	Bongaigaon	2.35
15.	Numaligarh Refinery Ltd.(NRL)	Numaligarh	3.00
16.	Mangalore Refinery & Petrochemicals Ltd. (MRPL)	Mangalore	9.69
17.	Tatipaka refinery (ONGC)	Andhra Pradesh	0.066
18.	Reliance Petroleum Ltd. (RPL). Pvt. Sector	Jamnagar	33.00
19.	Reliance Petroleum Ltd. (SEZ). Pvt. Sector (production started in Jan. 2009)	Jamnagar	29.00
20.	Essar Oil Limited (EOL). Pvt. Sector (Production started in Dec. 2006)	Jamnagar	10.50
	Total		179.956

*Million Metric Tonnes per Annum.

Notes: CPCL and BRPL are subsidiaries of IOC, NRL is subsidiary of BPC, MRPL is subsidiary of ONGC and KRL is merged with BPCL w.e.f. 21 August, 2006.

Source: Website, Executive Summary, Outcome Budge 2010-11, GoI, Ministry of Petroleum and Natural Gas.

self-sufficiency in petroleum products to the extent of 70 percent. However, towards the end of the 80s the situation began worsening. Due to expanding demand and lack of resources, created at least partially by the policy of shunning the private sector to take up exploration at the required scale, the index of self- reliance came down to 30 percent at the beginning of the present decade and this has declined further to just 23 percent at the end of the decade. The government was forced to open the door to the private sector in late 1980s and ensure a level playing field in the upstream (exploration and extraction) sector between the private and the public sector companies. This policy has already borne fruit. The pace of exploration has gathered momentum, so much so that both the Indian state-owned firms and private firms are now investing heavily in oil and gas fields abroad towards the objective of hydrocarbon security.

The major refineries coming up in 1990s are Panipat Refinery (Haryana) of IOC and Mangalore Refinery (Karnataka) which is currently a majority

Table 2.2: Planned Capacity Expansion during XIth Five Year Plan

Sl.No.	*Name of the Company*	*Location of the Refinery*	*Capacity (MMTPA)**
1.	Indian Oil Corporation Limited (IOCL)	Panipet	3.00
2.	IOCL	Haldia	1.50
3.	Hindustan Petroleum Corporation Limited (HPCL)	Mumbai	2.40
4.	HPCL	Visakhapatnam	2.50
5.	Chennai Petroleum Corporation Limited (CPCL)	Manali	1.60
6.	BPCL, Kochi Refineries Ltd. (KRL)	Kochi	2.0
7.	Mangalore Refinery & Petrochemicals Ltd. (MRPL)	Mangalore	5.31
8.	Oil and Natural Gas Corporation (ONGC)	Tatipaka	0.066
9.	Essar Oil Limited (EOL). Pvt. Sector	Vadinar	5.50
	Total		23.876

*Excludes those already shown in Table 2.1.
Source: Website, Executive summary, Outcome Budget 2010-11, Refineries in India, Ministry of Petroleum and Natural Gas, GoI.

held subsidiary of ONGC. Other refineries are Numaligarh (Assam), a majority held subsidiary of BPCL and a small refinery of ONGC at Tatipaka (Andhra Pradesh). These last two refineries have been commissioned in 2000 and 2001 respectively.

Outside the public sector, there were very major developments in the private sector during the 90s and later. Reliance Industries Limited has set up Asia's largest refinery with capacity of 33 MMPTA at Jamnagar, Gujrat, the first phase of which started production in late 1999 and then the company set up a second refinery (SEZ) in the same district with an installed capacity of 29 MMPTA. The SEZ refinery started production in 2009. Over and above this Essar Oil Limited set up a refinery of capacity 10.5 MMPTA at Vadinar, Gujrat, in 2006. The refineries of India with their present capacities as in October, 2009, are shown in Table 2.1. Tables 2.2 and 2.3 present the capacity expansion schemes of existing refineries and the schedule of new grassroots refineries due to come up during the eleventh five year plan period. As a result of the huge initiative in refinery capacity creation India is presently a net exporter of petroleum products and is expected to remain so in the near future in spite of rapidly expanding domestic demand for petroleum products.

Table 2.3: Grassroots Refineries Coming up during XIth Five Year Plan*

Sl.No.	*Name of the Company*	*Location of the Refinery*	*Capacity (MMTPA)**
1.	Indian Oil Corporation Limited (IOCL)	Paradip, Orissa	15.00
2.	Bharat Oman Refineries Limited (BORL)	Bina, MP	6.00
3.	Hindustan Mittal Energy Limited (HMEL)	Bhatinda, Punjab	9.00
4	Essar Oil Limited (EOL)	Jamnagar, Gujrat	18.00
5.	Nagarjuna Oil Corporation Limited (NOCL)	Cuddalore, Tamil Nadu	6.00
	Total		54.00

Excludes those already shown in Table 2.1
Source: Website, Executive Summary, Outcome Budget 2010–11, Ministry of Petroleum and Natural Gas, GoI.

The domestic refining capacity in the country as on March 31, 2009, was 177.97 MMTPA out of which 72.47 MMTPA was in the private sector.

The refineries are now producing cleaner fuels in line with the norms of the National Auto Fuel Policy which sets out a road map for supply of greener (Euro III and Euro IV grade) MS and HSD (petrol and diesel) to different cities of the country. In order to meet their targets the Oil Marketing Companies (OMCs) have undertaken and implemented several modernization projects.

Majority of the public sector oil units are either Navaratna or Mini Ratna companies. Major projects of these oil units are monitored by the Ministry Monitoring Cell since early 80s through Memorandum of Understandings negotiated with the units with regard to targets to be attained by the units. The Ministry in its turn has set for itself the guiding principles as set out in the document Hydrocarbon Vision-2025 of the government of India. The long term vision highlights energy security, cleaner products and greener practice, continuous upgradation of efficiency viewed from the global standard and promotion of competition within the industry, and strategic and defence considerations.

2.3 A Broader Perspective

Expansion of refining capacity in India started almost immediately after independence but substantial expansion of crude production had to wait for two decades. Thus, during the first two decades the index of self reliance[1] was very low. India imported more than ninety percent of the petroleum needs of the country. This did not seem to be a great burden as prices were low and stable. In 1970–71 India's gross import of petroleum crude and products as a percentage of total exports was less than 10%. In such circumstances prices were naturally set on an import parity basis. Domestic production of crude picked up over the 1960s and the degree of self reliance rose up to thirty-five percent in early 1970s with promise of further rise. At this stage came the first international oil price shock of 1973–74. Rising oil prices became a serious problem, so much so that the import bill for petroleum accounted for almost 80% of total export earnings in 1980–81. Since some products like kerosene (for lighting and cooking) and diesel (for mass transport) are related to poor man's utility, the government necessarily feels pressure to keep their prices low

[1]It is the ratio of crude oil produced in the country (as a percentage) to total crude oil necessary to meet domestic consumption of petroleum oil products.

and stable. With some degree of self reliance (table 2.4) and further encouraging prospects in this respect, as is reflected in the improvement in the degree of self reliance over the next decade, the government was impelled to act. Thus came the Administered Price Mechanism (APM) which ruled for almost three decades before being abandoned only in the present decade.

Table 2.4: Petroleum: Production and Self-Reliance

Year	*Crude Production*	*Refinery Throughput*	*Net Import of Crude and Pol* Products*		*Gross Pol* imports as % of India's Total exports*	*Index of Self Reliance*
			Quantity	*Value*		
1947–48	0.25	0.25	NA	NA	NA	9
1950–51	0.26	2.26	NA	NA	NA	7
1960–61	0.45	6.13	7.71	53	NA	5
1970–71	6.82	18.38	12.43	132	8.9	35
1980–81	10.51	25.84	23.50	5258	78.5	32
1990–91	33.02	51.77	26.71	9775	33.1	56
1995–96	35.17	58.74	44.24	22263	22.7	44
2000–01	32.43	103.44	75	70353	38.3	30
2005–06	32.19	130.11	89.39	149700	43.7	26
2008–09	33.51	161	114.53	291471	53.8	23

* Pol: Petroleum oil and lubricants.

Source: Indian Petroleum and Natural Gas Statistics, GoI, 2008 and 2009.

We have already seen that refining capacity expanded rapidly almost all through (Figure 2.1). Compound annual growth rate of crude throughput in Indian refineries (both public and private) was close to 4 percent over the last five decades. Refinery production balanced domestic consumption in 2002–03 and since then India is a surplus producer. But the worry remains regarding self reliance. One prognosis is that India's degree of self reliance will decline from the present level of 20% to just 10% in 2030.[2]

[2] See World Energy Outlook 2009, International Energy Agency, OECD, Paris.

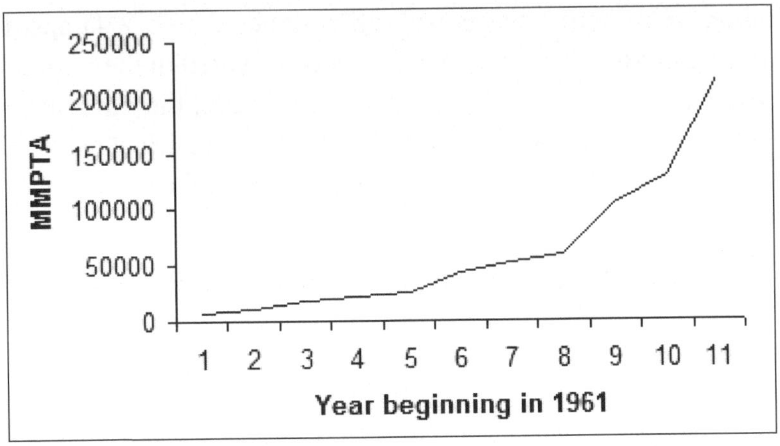

Fig. 2.1: Quinquennial Crude Throughput in Indian Refineries

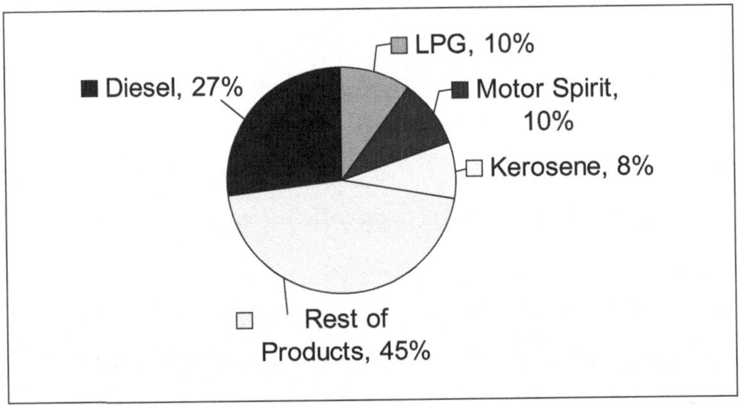

Fig. 2.2: Sensitive Products in Total Production of PSCs: 2008–09

Refineries produce several products; some are sensitive in the sense that their price changes directly affect the common people. Such products are kerosene, diesel, LPG and motor spirit. Kerosene is the source of light in large parts of the country even a century and half after it was invented as such by a Polish pharmacist and started to be used in kerosene lamps. LPG is supposed to be a merit good as it helps conservation and better use of biomass fuels. Diesel is used in mass transport of both passengers and goods. Motor spirit is used mainly in cars. Proportion of different petroleum products in the total production of 2008-09 in India is shown in the pie chart (Figure 2.2) above. Steadily rising demand for petroleum products is a concomitant to modern economic growth. The government is in constant struggle to ensure adequate supply at reasonably stable prices; but in a losing battle it seems to be learning to live with unstable prices.

Chapter 3

Industry Structure and Pricing of Products

The first reason for intervention is to protect poor consumers so that they may afford kerosene for lighting, which is a necessity for those who do not have access to electricity.

Kirit Parikh Committee, 2010

Introduction

Oil and natural gas, also known as hydrocarbons, meets 45% of primary energy requirement (i.e., energy requirement met through transformation of natural resources into different forms of energy) of the country at present. The Ministry of Petroleum and Natural Gas (MoPNG) has the responsibility of exploration and production of oil and natural gas (and also their imports), their refining and marketing. The Indian oil economy can be divided into 3 (overlapping) sub-sectors:

1. Oil and Gas Exploration and Production
2. Oil Refining
3. Marketing (Gas and Refinery Products)

Exploration and production (i.e., extraction) are referred to as upstream activities while refining and further processing related to petrochemical industry are downstream activities. The major players in the oil sector generally combine both upstream and down stream activities to realize synergy. Nevertheless, companies differ with respect to their focus.

3.1 The Major Players: Upstream Sector

There are three central public sector enterprises (PSCs) with their focus on exploration and extraction of crude. These are Oil & Natural Gas Corporation Ltd. (ONGC), incorporated in 1956, ONGC Videsh Ltd. (OVL), incorporated in 1965 and Oil India Ltd. (OIL), incorporated in 1981. In terms of turnover ONGC accounts for more than 80% of total of the upstream sector while the other two companies are of comparable size as in the financial year 2008-09. OVL is, in fact, a subsidiary of ONGC, the premier Indian company engaged in production and exploration of hydrocarbons, which aims at being a world-class company integrated in energy business with dominant Indian leadership and global presence. ONGC is incorporated in several energy joint ventures and it has a prominent subsidiary—Mangalore Refinery and Petrochemicals (MRPL). This account shows that in spite of having a basic focus in exploration and extraction of oil, the company has a wide and integrated vision.

OVL was originally Hydrocarbons India Pvt. Ltd., incorporated in 1965, and later renamed as ONGC Videsh Ltd. in 1989. It is a 100% subsidiary of ONGC and was set up with the objective to undertake the international business of production and exploration of hydrocarbons for its parent company. It operated abroad in a large number of projects over a wide range of countries of Asia, Africa and Latin America. The company plays an important role from the point of view of the Hydrocarbon Vision – 2025 of the government of India. OIL, on the other hand, was set up with the narrow objective to manage the oilfields of Naharkatiya of Assam but with the passage of time it has spread the boundaries of its operation far within the country and beyond. It is focused on exploration and production of crude and gas but it also undertakes the important task of transportation of crude and gas.

Realizing the widening gap between the demand and indigenous supply of oil & gas in the country and the inadequacy of national oil companies in this respect due to scarcity of resources and non-availability of appropriate technology the government of India opened up the sector of exploration & production of oil & gas to the world community through New Exploration Licensing Policy (NELP). ONGC could not venture into deep waters of East coast in all earnest due to its limitations with technology. The private sector came forward to open up the east coast deep waters for commercial exploitation. Credit goes to the private companies like Cairn, Essar Oil and Reliance Industries Limited (RIL). These companies are operating now in a big way and with a wide focus.

3.2 The Major Players: Downstream Sector

The major operators in the public sector focused to the downstream sector are given below[1] along with the size of their turnover (in Rs. Crores) in 2008–09.

---

[1]*Source:* Public Enterprises Survey, 2008-09, GoI.

	Company	*Turnover (Rs. crores)*
1.	Indian Oil corporation Ltd (IOCL)	329731
2.	Bharat Petroleum Corporation Ltd. (BPCL)	145392
3.	Hindustan Petroleum Corporation (HPCL)	116427
4.	Mangalore Refinery & Petrochemicals Ltd (MRPL)	42718
5.	Chennai Petroleum Corporation Ltd. (CPCL)	36534
6.	Gail (India) Ltd.	24292
7.	Numaligarh Refinary Ltd.	8853

We have already discussed the origins of these companies, except that of GAIL, in Chapter 2. GAIL was incorporated in 1984 with the objective of optimizing the use of natural gas and its fractions. It does not operate in the field of oil refining. Another big player in the field of oil refining, Kochi Refineries Ltd. (KRL), has been merged with BPCL with retrospective effect from April, 2004, through an order dated August 2006.

All the three behemoths—IOCL, BPCL and HPCL—are refiners as well as marketers of refinery products. They market not only their own products, but also products of other refiners, including those in the private sector. BPCL has ventured into the field of oil and gas exploration through a subsidiary—Bharat Petro Resources Ltd.—to ensure supply security and hedge against price fluctuations. Both IOCL and HPCL operate a wide network of pipelines for transportation of crude and refined products. They are focused to refining and marketing. The oldest oil marketing company of India, Indo-Burma Petroleum Company ltd. used to be operative in the marketing arena until it was merged with the IOCL in May 2007.

The three remaining smaller companies are each a subsidiary of a large company. As already stated, MRPL is a subsidiary of ONGC since 2003. It is focused to refining as well as production of petrochemicals. The company has ambitions of expanding its direct marketing business. CPCL is a subsidiary of the IOCL, and is focused to refining. NRL is a subsidiary of the BPCL. It is focused to refining and is also increasingly gearing up to marketing its products in a large way.

Thus marketing of petroleum products is basically the responsibility of the three behemoths that are also focused to refining and diversified to other activities like exploration and transportation of oil to realize synergy.

Smaller companies naturally have narrower focus. KPCL was there till 2006 when it was merged with BPCL with retrospective effect. MRPL has emerged as a significant player only after 2003 while NRL started operation late in 2000. CPCL is the other relatively small company focused to refining. Focus of our study in chapter 7 is comparison of technical efficiency in refining operations of all the companies in the public sector engaged in refining. Clearly, a serious comparison is possible only if the different operations of the companies can be somehow segregated in terms of use of resources. We have discussed these issues in Chapter 6.

3.3 Price Determination

Prices of petroleum products used to be determined by the Administered Pricing Mechanism (APM) until it was fully dismantled in 2002. The APM has its roots in the early seventies when Shipping Corporation of India (SCI) took a loan from the World Bank to purchase oil carriers. The World Bank then recommended a 'cost plus' pricing formula to SCI for freight calculation. The same principle in the name of 'retention concept' was later (1976) introduced to crude and petroleum products pricing system. The Oil Pricing Committee (OPC) in 1976, recommended the discontinuance of the import parity based pricing and sowed the seeds for total regulation of the oil industry in India, through a virtually unanchored APM. As per the suggestions of OPC, APM ushered in a regime of a sort of cost-plus pricing based on domestic cost of production (retention price), which would take into account the delivered cost of crude, refinery operating cost and a reasonable guaranteed return on capital employed. Accordingly, the price of indigenous crude was based on operating cost plus 15% post tax return on capital employed. And oil refineries and marketing companies calculated the price of their products on the basis of operating cost plus 12% return post tax on net worth.[2] The other important component of APM – a complicated pricing formula – is "cross subsidization mechanism".

Cross-subsidized petroleum products competed with other energy sources like coal. Thus low priced kerosene has replaced vegetable oil for illuminating lamps and coal for cooking, subsidized LPG has become an essential household fuel, long distance trucks fed with cheap diesel easily

[2] Capital employed is the sum of fixed and working capital. Net Worth is paid-up capital plus share application money pending allotment and reserves less accumulated losses and Deferred Revenue Expenditure not written off.

competed with the railways in freight movement and subsidized naptha made the coal technology unviable for fertilizer production. This pricing policy backed with elaborate distribution system has made the entire economy almost completely dependent on petroleum products. The 'retention concept' on the other hand did not allow the PSUs with guaranteed returns to become sick.

Table 3.1: Retail Prices of Selected Petroleum Products in Delhi

Year	*Petrol*	*Diesel*	*Kerosene*	*LPG*
1975*	3.27	1.11	1.08	NA
1980	5.11	2.28	1.54	43.53
1985	7	3.47	2.18	51.35
1990	9.84	4.08	2.25	57.61
1995	16.8	6.98	2.57	93.28
2000	26.7	14.56	5.55	196.55
2005	37.99	28.22	9.02	294.75
2009	40.62	30.86	9.22	179.7

* Data for 1975 relate to the month of January though for other years the relevant date is April 1.

Source: Indian Petroleum and Natural Gas Statistics, 2008 and 2009.

Faced with international price fluctuations for crude oil and its products on the one hand, and declining index of self reliance in the sector since mid-1980s on the other, the government had no way of stopping the steady draining of the exchequer in the form of oil subsidy. The Oil Pool mechanism underlying the APM was based on the idea that prices somehow would rule at the long term rolling average levels so that in times of international price shoot-up the Pool would subsidize and it would be replenished when international prices deep. Thus ultimately cost increases of refineries are supposed to be passed on to the consumers after some smoothening. But this mechanism fails when price rises are phenomenal and sustained as the reality has been mostly. So, in effect, the refineries suffered due to irregular and only partial payments from the oil pool which was proving to be a great drag on government resources in spite of considerable hikes in retail prices of petroleum products (Table 3.1, and Fig. 3.1) from time to time.

The APM was finally dismantled in 2002. But that proved to be a temporary respite as international oil prices again shot up phenomenally.

The situation has been summarized by the Kirit Parikh Committee (2010): "In March, 2002... the price of the Indian basket of crude oil in the international market was US $ 23.3/barrel: it rose to US $ 39.2/barrel in 2004-5. Since then, the unprecedented roller-coaster movement of oil prices in the international market can be judged from the following facts. It took 3 years for the oil prices to double from US $ 36/barrel in July 2004 to US $ 72/barrel in July 2007, but took only one year to further double to around US $ 144/barrel in July 2008. Far more precipitous was the fall in prices since then when within a matter of five months, in December 2008 oil prices fell back to July 2004 level. Since then oil prices have bounced back to US $ 75/barrel in December 2009." Oil subsidy again soared and slumped. The government continues to grapple with a solution.

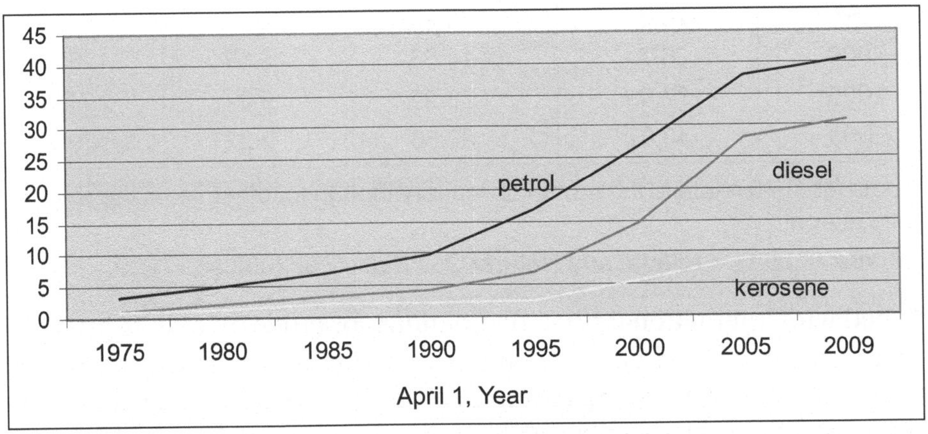

Fig. 3.1: Retail Prices of Selected Petroleum Products in Delhi

As far as refineries are concerned their financial position did suffer due to the irregularity and uncertainty of payment of compensation. Further, it was being felt increasingly that guaranteed profits under the APM were sapping the competitive spirit of the state-owned oil companies leading to inefficient operations jeopardizing the prospect of resource generation and long term growth. The oil Industry Restructuring Group (R-Group), set up in 1995 to study the overall oil scenario (both domestic and international) and suggest the future course of action, submitted its report in September 1996. As regards the downstream refining sector, apart from suggesting the incorporation of new refineries in private and joint sectors to enhance the total refining capacity of the country, the R-Group advocated measures for improvement of the operational efficiency, better product mix (that matches the demand-mix of the petro-products), more value-added products and upgradation to state-of-art technology for the existing refineries. Interestingly, the R-Group found considerable scope for improvement in operational efficiency in the refineries (i.e, reduction in fuel loss from the present level of 7% to 5–6%, less consumption of auxiliary fuel, increased manpower productivity), achieving a better product mix and improvement of distillate yield from the level of 70% to 80% through technology upgradation.

With the discontinuation of the APM the competitive spirit was restored as the companies did no longer enjoy protection of returns on their costs and investments. Almost coinciding with the discontinuation of the APM private refiners appeared on the scene in a big way; this must had revved up the competitive spirit. The fact that the government backtracked on the principle of market determined prices two years later did not really undo the competitive spirit as the retention concept was not restored, though it did put the PSCs in financial uncertainty. In fact, one may argue this put further pressure on the PSEs to heighten efficiency of operations. Indeed, in Chapter 7 we will find strong evidence of improved technical efficiency of oil refining PSCs after the dismantling of the APM.

Chapter 4

Technical Efficiency and its Measurement

As your bright and tiny spark, /Lights the traveler in the dark,
Though I know not what you are, / Twinkle, twinkle, little star.

Nursery Rhyme "The Star" by Jane Taylor, 1806

Introduction

An economist's world is different from that of a natural scientist. When an economist talks of efficiency in production s/he is not really concerned whether the most sophisticated machine is being operated to obtain the product though this may be important in many cases; nor is s/he always interested in churning out the most sophisticated product. It is common knowledge that art-films of great sophistication are often uneconomic as they fail to make a mark in the box-office. Similarly, there are highly sophisticated scientific technologies shining in the laboratories but unable to hit the market for lack of demand. For economic production the two primary concerns are market demand that generates revenue and market supply that is determined by cost. Though the economic reality of production organization may be viewed as a continuum of possibilities, economists seek to portray the underlying essence by the concept of profit maximization which principle subsumes cost minimization as its dual problem.

4.1 The Concept of Efficiency in Production

Profit maximization must be ruthlessly pursued for survival in a Darwinian process when competition is perfect; but otherwise, in the real world, there may be cases of laxity in that pursuit giving rise to sub-optimal use of resources for lack of incentive or distractions caused by other non-profit motives. This seems to be a rather common but imprecise statement associated with the concept of "X-inefficiency"

(Leibenstein, 1966).[1] Thus, when a public sector unit is set up in a backward region based on criteria broader than technical efficiency of the particular plant, it may lead to use of resources not guided by the principle of profit maximization, thus leading to technical ineffi-ciency or X-inefficiency. This may be apparent when the unit is compared to the performance of other similar units not subjected to economic considerations. This inefficiency violates the technical objec-tive, viewed simply, of producing the highest output given the quantity of input or, what is its dual problem, obtaining a given output using the smallest quantity of input, both strictly defined in the context of profit maximization.[2] The objective of achieving technical efficiency, which may be viewed as avoidance of waste, is enshrined in (though not implied by) the assumptions of profit maximization or cost minimization. A deviation from this objective must not be random; that must have reason. If the reason is to be integrated into our analysis it may need a redefinition of output. Thus if the objective of an unit is to generate profit as well as some benefit to the adjoining locality the benefit should also be considered as part of the appropriate concept of product. Defining such a concept is often a tricky problem and, so, avoided.[3] Thus deviation from single minded pursuit of profit maximization would contribute to measured technical inefficiency.

---

[1] The concept has been criticized (Stigler, 1976) for not being rigorously specified. Indeed, this type of inefficiency may not necessarily be related to any incompetence of factors of production and might be explained if the specification of the technology along with the actual structural and behavioural characteristics supporting non-profit-maximizing behaviour could be fully and satisfactorily modeled. This deficiency of economic theory hinders a precise explanation of inefficiency defined in terms of predefined concepts of output and input.

[2] To keep the language simple without losing the essence forget for the moment that there may be several inputs and products. In our discussion below we have used the terms output and product almost interchangingly though output may take the form of several products. Product may also take the interpretation of value-added in specific contexts.

[3] Thus when a plant is set up in a backward region on some ground external to the pure economic interest of the firm concerned, achievement of the external objective must be accounted for in a just evaluation of the firm's performance and this may need a redefinition of the variables (Sen, 1983, Bhattcharya and Datta, 2004).

An economist has no partiality for any particular resource — be it a machine, a part of the plant or labour. All resources are obtainable for money which has alternative uses. Money is used on resources that are classified as labour, capital, etc. These different resources may be substitutable among themselves in different degrees and have different marginal productivities. Thus while resources or inputs of production have several dimensions, a production process most often turns out several products and there often exists substitutability among them too. A manager with economic optimization as the goal, therefore, must decide on both the input combination and the output combination keeping in view marginal productivities of resources and marginal revenues of products. And here comes the question of economic efficiency, the resultant of technical and allocative efficiencies.

The problem becomes one of purely technical efficiency when we abstract from the allocation aspect. Consider a fixed coefficient technology producing a fixed combination of products; so, we need not bother about substitutability between inputs or choice of the combination of products. Thus, for all practical purposes, we can talk of a single composite input giving a single composite output. In this case the challenge to the manager is to attain full utilization of the technical potential of the input and challenge to the researcher is to somehow measure the slack in attainment. We may note that the problem in this simple form may be studied solely from the technical point of view without imposition of any behavioural assumption of profit maximization or cost minimization though, of course, the behavioural assumptions give a motive to the attainment of technical efficiency. We have already indicated that there may be a slack in the attainment because of several reasons including incompetence and lack of incentive. But the problem to the researcher is how to know the state of full attainment, or the frontier, from which to measure distance, or inefficiency, of actual attainment.

It should be clear from the above discussion that the consideration of technical efficiency bypasses the question of allocative efficiency and this bypass is fully justified when the technology is characterized by fixed coefficients; but when that is not so the question of economic efficiency is a much broader and appropriate one for judging the economic performance of a firm. Since the whole question of allocation, be it related to inputs or products, is based on cost and revenue considerations and is, therefore, related to the set of relative prices, the measurement of economic efficiency must be based on price-data apart from quantities. Thus we need a larger set of information compared to what we need for evaluating technical efficiency. The problem is compounded by the fact that prices are often highly volatile.[4] This is particularly so in the petroleum industry and we will come back to this point again in the next chapter. Indeed, research output is not costless. To obtain greater information in the form of a broader concept, the economic efficiency, we need a larger set of information which increases the level of difficulty of the task. So, as we have to limit our choice in almost every sphere of real life, (in order to remain focused) we will mainly limit ourselves here to the discussion of technical efficiency and issues related to that.

4.2 Necessary Abstraction of the Reality

A researcher has a set of observations on products and inputs. Nobody tells him how much more of different products could be had with the given set of inputs or, how much less of different inputs could have been adequate for the same set of products. We will confine ourselves to the first problem, i.e., output based measures. Let us consider a single product and two inputs – labour and capital. This makes matters easier to grasp conceptually though for empirical applications this intensifies the problem of aggregation of disparate variables which must be formed into groups and reduced to indices. We will discuss this point further in the specific context of petroleum refineries in the next chapter.

Measuring efficiency essentially involves visualization of an optimum and then studying how the optimum is being approached. Thus the concept of production frontier is relevant. We write $Y=F(K, L)$, where Y, K and L refer to indices of product, capital and labour. Thus, if we have observations on the variables, a suitable functional form for the production frontier can be estimated provided the observations belong to the frontier; i.e., the production programme of each firm is fully efficient or

[4] This complicates collection of data as well as their relevance since production process is generally not amenable to tweaking too frequently.

optimal.[5] To make appeal to a coherent theory of producer behaviour the frontier is characterized by positive and diminishing marginal productivities. So, we have:

$$Y = F(K, L),\ F_K, F_L > 0, F_{KK}, F_{LL} < 0 \qquad \ldots (4.1)$$

The maintained assumption here is that the same frontier is relevant for all plants.[6] To the extent the playing field is not level – say, the different firms face varying degrees of regulations – or operating conditions are not reasonably identical in the sense that infrastructural or technological benefits are not equally realized, disadvantages will be reflected in inefficiency even if the firm concerned achieves the best under the constraints. So, what we really try to find out is not just managerial efficiency within a given plant but the overall efficiency (without discounting for practical constraints) that is relevant for survival in business. A smooth production function is an abstraction and our endeavour is to get the essence of the multi-dimensional reality through abstractions. The beauty of reasonable abstraction is that it generates new insights and ideas, as we will find some instances below. But one

[5] Note that we have excluded intermediate input from this representation. Obviously, its implications like its separability in the representation of the production function and the definition of the product as value added must be kept in mind if the representation is to be used (Arrow, 1974). When intermediate input is not separable from primary inputs use of this form is not permitted for an industry or a sub-sector of the economy. However, for economy wide studies (of closed economies) we may ignore intermediate inputs as they may be assumed to be generated by the overall production process.

[6] Strictly speaking, existence of a generalized production function requires that all the firms of different sizes and the industry have production functions that are identical up to a constant multiplier (Fisher, 1965). While it is a very strict restriction, mere existence does not justify the assumption of its being unchanging over time. Thus, there is no theoretical reason why the coefficients of the production function should be constant over time or should be the same across firms. The whole idea behind abstraction is attempting at obtaining reasonable summary statistics when it is not possible or convenient to capture actual variations in characteristics under study. But even this idea is not scientifically established (Felipe and Fisher, 2008). It reminds one of Lewis Caroll: "Twinkle, Twinkle little bat How I wonder what you are at! Up above the world you fly, Like a tea-tray in the sky".

has always to be conscious about the possible pitfalls and limitations of interpretations.

To illustrate from the petroleum refining process, a typical modern petroleum refining plant is an integrated system of 10 to 15 separate units with distinct designs, equipments and structures and functions. Apart from the differences in designs and structures, there are differences in product compositions. Further, plants often have location specific requirements. A refinery located in a densely populated area, like BPCL and HPCL plants in Mumbai, will probably have to make more stringent security arrangements compared to those located in relatively secluded places. The implication is that investment required in this regard will be higher for such a plant compared to one located outside cities or towns and this higher investment will not be reflected in higher output.

Similarly, serious problem arises with respect to investments related to environmental norms. Many refineries make such investments (like in sulphur recovery plants) either directly to help environment without any implication for their products (except recovery of some low-value sulfur) or indirectly to improve the quality of product (making it more environment friendly). Thus Euro III or Euro IV grade petrol are obtained at a higher cost that may perhaps be reflected in higher price, but the investment required for the purpose does not generate higher physical quantity of product. Reality being so varied, no two plants are

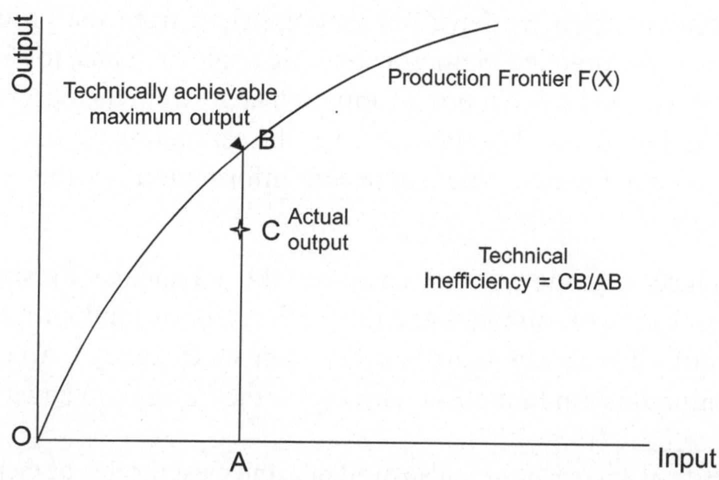

Fig. 4.1: Technical Efficiency with Non-Stochastic Frontier

identical. It is often said that each plant has its own character. Yet, our measurement of efficiency is about comparison among such plants. Clearly, one has to be extremely cautious in carrying interpretation of results beyond generalities.

Now, given the frontier, or the technical maximum, technical efficiency is indicated by the distance of actual achievement of a firm from the technically achievable maximum. The idea is easily illustrated by Fig. 4.1. To make possible presentation in two dimensions we consider one composite input to produce one composite output. With OA input AB is technically achievable maximum output though the firm gets only AC. This gives the proportion of achievement lag to the full potential to be CB/AB, which is defined as technical inefficiency. In practical applications the problem is that C is observed but B is not. So, how does one get the frontier and calculate inefficiency? Sophisticated statistical techniques are available to do this. We discuss brief outlines of one most commonly implemented approach—the stochastic frontier approach (SFA)—below with the objective of giving an intuitive idea of the approach and its limitations.

Let us go back to our production frontier (4.1). We have noted that this representation does not leave any scope for any inefficiency. Only a 100% efficient firm will lie on the frontier. But we suspect that most firms are inefficient in different degrees and we do not know which firm, if any, is fully efficient. So, in fact, our observations generally do not lie on the frontier which we have not distinguished from the production function as is the practice in microeconomic analysis. Thus, to visualize the frontier we need some more information apart from the observations on inputs and products. The innovation in the estimation process in SFA is about supplementing this supposed information to the existing observations.

We introduce a random error term to take advantage of statistical hypothesis testing of estimates and justify the error by random shocks on output from all possible sources other than inefficiency.[7] Apart from incorporating this random noise term (v_i for the ith firm, in equation-4.2

[7] Non-statistical approaches are also available, the most notable of them being the Data Envelopment Analysis (Ray, 2004; Coelli, Rao and Battese, 1998).

below)[8] in the production function the trick that econometricians resort to, in order to estimate inefficiencies, is the assumption that efficiency is a random phenomenon in the sense that its incidence is not correlated with output or factor employment. Further, since inefficiency can only pull a plant below its frontier, efficiency is generally less than, but at the most equal to one. A 100% efficient plant has an efficiency factor equal to one. In the presence of producer specific random shocks representing the efficiency factor (TE_i for the ith firm), the observed output may be written in terms of the stochastic production frontier as:

$$Y_i = F(X_i, \beta).\exp\{v_i\}.TE_i \qquad \ldots(4.2)$$

Actual observations will still lie below the estimated production function, $F(X_i, \beta)$, except in exceptional cases when a highly efficient firm also gets a favourable random shock (error) from the environment broadly defined (may be an unusually favourable weather in agriculture). Slight inefficiency does not pull it down significantly but favourable random error pushes it up beyond the production function. In diagram-2 such an exceptional case is depicted as the third observation from the left.

In (4.2) we have altered the representation of the production function a bit in order to explicitly show the parameters of the production function to be estimated. In this form Y is the output and X is the vector of factors of production while β represents the vector of parameters (coefficients) of the production function represented by F; and v is a white noise disturbance affecting the production process of the ith firm as mentioned earlier. Equation 4.2 defines technical efficiency, TE_i, as the ratio of observed output (Y_i) to maximum feasible (full efficiency) output in an environment characterized by the random error exp (v_i).[9] Because of the random error the frontier is no more a fixed one. It is a stochastic frontier.

---

[8] Over and above this it is assumed that the random shock is characterized by a normally distributed random variable with zero mean and variance to be determined.

[9] The random variables $v_{i's}$ are assumed to be independently and identically distributed normal variables with mean zero and constant unknown variance and are assumed to follow a specific distribution. The pioneering work of Aigner, Lovell and Schmidt (1977) assumed $v_{i's}$ to be independent of the random efficiency variables which were also assumed to follow specific distribution patterns. For further discussion see chapter 5.

The analysis can be further extended to take account of several observations over time for each firm and if the time period involved is long it may be inappropriate to take technical efficiency to be time-invariant. That brings further complication to the estimation process, the term TE_i in (4.2) will now be subject to change over time; we may now write it as TE_{it} though in the actual estimation process it has to be given an explicit expression involving time.

Assumption of a distributional form for technical efficiency allows us to estimate the required parameters following maximum-likelihood estimation procedure. It is possible to estimate technical efficiencies of individual plants (Jondrow *et al.* 1982) on probabilistic basis; as conditional expectations. The challenge often lies in obtaining the relevant data[10] and refining it suitably. It should be emphasized here that the estimates of efficiency are subject to the distributional assumption but they are normally consistent in the sense that reliability is greater when we have larger number of firms and large number of observations on each firm.

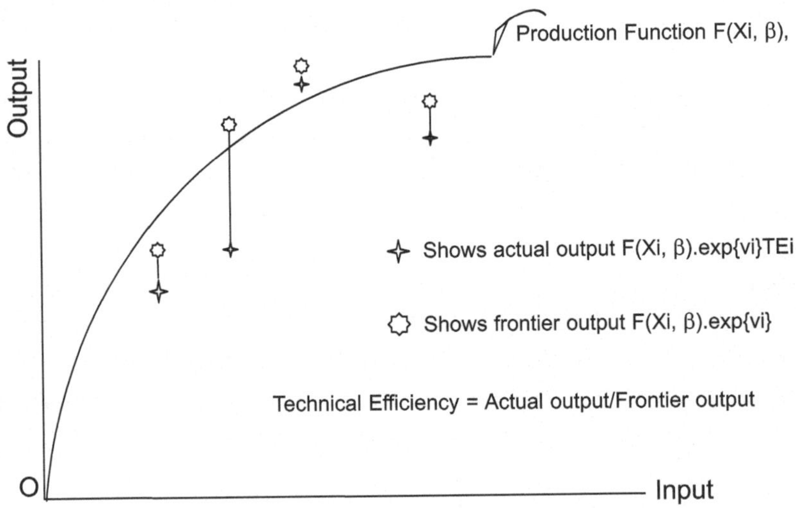

Fig. 4.2: Technical Efficiency with Stochastic Frontier

While the assumptions are sought to be given an intuitive appeal to the extent possible, it goes without saying that they are not accurate reflections of the reality and the estimates are subject to the validity of the assumptions (which are specified in further detail in Chapter 5). It is

[10] Normally panel data, i.e., data on several plants over a number of years, are needed.

possible to make alternative assumptions regarding the form of the production frontier and distribution of efficiency. Econometricians mostly prefer the most flexible forms to get the best fit with observations. If the estimates vary significantly so as to alter conclusions when assumptions are altered, estimates are not robust and so, not reliable. Monte-Carlo studies,[11] however, show that the major conclusions are generally robust under standard alternative assumptions regarding the forms of the production frontier and the distribution functions for efficiency (Kumbhakar and Lovell, 2000, pp. 106–7). This means that even though the estimates would vary with alteration of assumptions, the variation would, generally, not be so much as to change the broad conclusion. This gives an important basis for proceeding with the exercise.[12] Nevertheless, the results warrant caution particularly with regard to precise conclusion regarding minute inefficiency characteristics of firms; like when two firms are rather close on their efficiency scores we should not put much weight on their relative ranks. Similarly, if efficiency is found to have a certain trend when a trans-log production function is assumed but not so when the form is Cobb-Douglas, it is probably better not to give the finding much importance unless tests establish one form of production function to give a decidedly better fit (statistically significant) compared to the other.[13]

---

[11]These are studies on several models using the same set of data to check how the conclusions vary.

[12]Problems regarding near-identifiability exists meaning imprecise and unstable estimates of model parameters (Bandyopadhyay and Das, 2008). This militates against minute comparison of inefficiency characteristics of firms.

[13]An alternative and common approach, left out of the present discourse, to the measurement of inefficiency is the Data Envelopement Analysis (DEA). One advantage with DEA is that it does not need a specification of the production function. It uses linear programming for estimation. This approach is non-parametric and does not account for random error due to environment and , so, it is free from distributional assumptions. Thus, while some of the criticisms against SFA do not affect DEA, it has the disadvantage of not being able to account for random production error even when it is important. Further, the DEA approach is not amenable to tests of hypotheses at any stage. Every econometrician knows, and we will find some examples in chapter 7, that tests of hypotheses are of great help in avoiding unfounded conclusions in some cases.

4.3 Total Factor Productivity and Technical Efficiency

A parallel, though different, concept is Total Factor Productivity (TFP). The concept is quite intuitive and found application much before it was elegantly presented.[14] Since partial productivities, like output per unit of labour or per-capita GDP, are part of the language of the common man; economists can naturally go a step further to find out output per unit of the totality of factors employed (Nadiri, 1970). The idea brings the challenge to construct an index of the totality of factors used in production and had got both theoreticians and empiricists among economists into a debate on how to do it best.[15] The debate still continues since there are complex questions like embodiment of technical progress which changes inputs themselves in the course of technical progress (Solow, 2001). Thus the quality of both capital and labour change making it difficult to measure a unit of total, or even a single, factor input comparable over time. In fact it has been claimed that the trend of quality adjusted price of machines can give an idea of the course of technical progress. Similar questions can be posed regarding labour input also. Thus, if technical progress is accounted for in measurement of inputs, to what extent does it remain to be accounted for separately in output? Thus the simple difference between the growth rates of output and quality adjusted total factor index may be misleading as a measure of technical change. A neat model may be filled out with data to churn out results which may not necessarily be so neat to interpret.

Ignoring the question of measurement of variables we can go back to our simplest explanatory technique. Consider a composite output, Y, and a composite input, X. So, productivity of the input is Y/X, which will be the total factor productivity as our input represents the totality of factors of production.[16] So, Total Factor Productivity Growth (TFPG) is the difference between the growth rates of output and totality of inputs. The

---

[14] The most elegant presentation of the concept is found in Solow (1957). For a survey of development of the concept see Griliches, 1996.

[15] Two very useful references on the subject are Hulten, 2001 and Greenwood and Jovanovic, 2001.

[16] We avoid the question of raw materials of production which adds to the complexity. This has been discussed in the context of oil refining in Chapter 7.

question is what the difference does really represent. It has casually been called a measure of technical change. But, as it is a residual it includes all sorts of influences that might affect *Y* and *X*; so, it includes, apart from the impact of changes in scientific technology, measurement errors, technical efficiency and any scale effect realized over time.

Again, to show the differences between the concepts dramatically, let us consider the case of a steady rate of improvement of technical efficiency, η, a return to scale parameter, μ, and a scale parameter, θ. Also, we assume a steady rate of technical change (Hicks neutral) at the rate λ. Then we may be permitted to write:

$$Y_t = e^{\lambda t} e^{\eta t} F(\theta_t X) = e^{\lambda t} e^{\eta t} \theta_t{}^{\mu} F(X) \qquad ...(4.3)$$

In this representation all parameters associated with time, t, are instruments of change in production. *F(X)* is a fixed quantity of output in the base period denoted by $t = 0$. So, $\theta_0 = 1$.Also, $\mu = 1$ for the case of constant returns to scale, greater or less than unity when returns to scale are increasing or decreasing respectively. So, total factor productivity is

$$(Y_t / \theta_t X) = e^{\lambda t} e^{\eta t} \theta_t{}^{\mu - 1} [F(X) / X] \qquad ...(4.4)$$

The expression within square bracket of (4) is a fixed base-year quantity. Taking logarithm and differentiating with respect to time one gets the growth rate of total factor productivity:

$$\text{TFPG} = \lambda + \eta + (\mu - 1) * \textit{rate of growth of } \theta \qquad ...(4.5)$$

Thus, when production is characterized by constant returns, TFPG is the sum of rate of technical change and rate of change of technical efficiency and, further, if technical change is absent then TFPG becomes equal to technical efficiency. However, for studies covering a substantial period of time it is inappropriate to assume absence of technical change. This message is not lost even when we do not represent technical change and efficiency the way we have done here.

It is clear from the above discussion that we really need to modify equation 4.2 to accommodate technical change as our discussion of technical efficiency does not leave any scope for technical change. Technical change is sometimes sought to be captured by incorporating a time variable in the production function. This gives the modified expression for (2) as: $Y_i = F(X_i, t, \beta).\exp\{v_i\}.TE_{it}$ ...(4.6)

In (4.6) the dimension of β is suitably modified to include the coefficient of the time variable in the production function. We should note that the technical efficiency term also incorporates a time element. As a result, this theoretical solution puts extra burden on the estimation procedure. The question is whether the estimation process can take account of multiple time variables in a way that can give the relevant coefficients the desired interpretations (technical efficiency and technical change). From this point of view it may sometimes be better to take a simpler expression for empirical implementation being fully conscious that the interpretation would also be much less refined. Thus if all the firms do not respond to technical change the same way, the progressive firms get to influence the frontier while the technologically backward firms' performances are compared with reference to the shifted frontier. This means that the measured inefficiency would also reflect failure to incorporate technical change, not just performance with reference to the level of technology the firms are actually operating under. Issues can be taken up with respect to returns to scale as well.

4.4 Data Generation

To explain the problem of data generation I will again take the example of oil refineries. For implementation of the TE model (4.2) we need data on output (Y), capital (K) and labour (L). All the three categories are heterogeneous. The challenge faced by the econometrician is to reduce each category into a single index number. The index number has to be such that it will not only add up the heterogeneous elements of a category; the quantity indices must also be comparable over time. In order to have some idea about the issues involved we will discuss the outlines of the case of measurement of the capital input. We do not discuss here the cases of measurement of output and labour as our objective here is to indicate the approach taken by economists and the difficulties faced by them in measuring economic efficiency. It bears an emphasis here that measurement of each variable is beset with problems peculiar to the variable.

Capital input refers to the assortment of machines and equipments as well as structures that form part in the plant. It has already been pointed out that a typical refinery contains 10 to 15 units; each unit is equipped with its distinctive parts. Thus without any exaggeration one can say that hundreds of equipments and structures form the capital stock of a refinery plant. The challenge is to find a quantity index.

Observable quantities are very often in money terms and at (historical) prices prevailing at the date of purchase. For economists prices contain a lot of information. Thus the value of a machine in a competitive market is taken as its true worth, i.e., its present discounted value of expected future returns. Since values can be added up, though not the physical units of heterogeneous equipments, the total market value of capital stock represents its true worth. So, market value at a particular point of time is taken to represent a certain physical units (quantity index) of capital stock.[17] The problem is that a plant contains machines of different vintages and there is practically no market for old machines. So, the market value of the whole stock, except at the date of commissioning is not available. It has to be estimated.[18]

Economists face the task of converting historical market values into values at the (constant) price level of some bench-mark year to enable quantitative comparison. But, since quantitative comparison is the objective, and relative prices as well as qualities change over time, the above exercise is of complicated. Here, we may need quality adjusted (Hedonic) price indices. But that is not all. A particularly perturbing problem is finding the appropriate rate of depreciation to be applied to machines installed in the past (Datta, 2006). It brings into consideration the difficult question of an age-efficiency profile for machines. It should by now be clear that estimation of capital input for the production frontier involves extremely complicated considerations even when we

---

[17] In fact, what is relevant is capital service. Going from stock to service (a flow) involves some intricate considerations briefly discussed in Chapter 5.

[18] What a great task we have accomplished here! It is one of the great conundrums of economics that many economists go on arguing like this in spite of the futility of such theoretical constructs as the aggregate production function, aggregate capital stock and the neo-classical marginal productivity theory. The concepts must have struck some chord in their brain at which the Cambridge capital controversy whittles away (for references see Filipe and Fisher, *op. cit.*).

possess data on investments at historical prices; but empirical studies are often made further difficult by the absence of even such data.

Let us again take the example of the petroleum refinery sector. For this sector published data relate to petroleum companies. Many companies like the Indian Oil Corporation Ltd., or the Hindusthan Petroleum Corporation Ltd., operate more than one refinery plant. What is required is plant level data because plants belonging to the same company may vary in efficiency. But life of the econometrician becomes even more hazardous because some companies engage in distribution of products while others do not. And distribution of products requires a capital intensive infrastructure which is not important for pure refiners (not engaging in distribution). Available data do not distinguish between capital required for production and that required for distribution. A serious researcher cannot work with available data without painstaking refinements.

4.5 Some Final Comments

The present state of knowledge regarding the measurement of economic efficiency is the result of research over at least the last six decades (Griliches, 1996). The present discussion portrays only one (but dominant) strand of research. It ignores one prominent development – the data envelopment analysis. The econometric techniques for the estimation of inefficiency using the stochastic frontier approach have been developed roughly over the last three decades.[19] Though we have outlined the measurement of output-oriented technical efficiency, a theoretically more satisfying approach is measurement of cost efficiency and its decomposition into input-based technical and allocative efficiency components. But data requirement for that approach is more demanding. What is more serious is that after the estimation of cost efficiency its decomposition into input oriented technical efficiency and allocative efficiency exposes the results to another level of challenge at the level of the conceptual development and unavoidable cumulative errors of measurement. From this point of view there may be some merit

[19] SFA is supposed to have originated in two papers published almost at the same time; these are Meeusen and van den Broeck (1977) and Aigner Lovell and Schmidt (1977).

in taking the relatively simple concept of technical efficiency as more practically relevant.

The econometric technique, once developed, reduces the estimation to a relatively simple task for the researcher thanks to the econometric software packages. The challenge lies in generation of the relevant data set. The brief discussion on the difficulties in measurement of capital input for oil refineries shows how complicated the task may be. We have discussed the serious problems associated with measurement of output and labour in Chapter 6. Sometimes even technically proficient researchers ignore these serious measurement aspects. But given the techniques, estimates can only be as good as the data. Also, we cannot be oblivious of the fact that econometrics do not solve problems left unresolved by theory. Thus, as we have seen, what we estimate as technical efficiency is not free from the effect of technical change. One must add to this the fact that a fully satisfactory data set is probably beyond the reach of the researcher in most cases while measurement errors and outliers among observations influence the position and shape of the frontier. These are points that bear weightage in any guarded conclusion.

In the light what we have said above, it is of some importance to note that the most efficient firm using the best technology has the greatest say in determining the frontier and so the efficiency scores obtained are only relative to such firms. Thus inclusion of new firms in a study can dramatically reduce, but cannot possibly improve significantly, the efficiency scores of existing firms. In the present study (in Chapter 7) we consider only the public sector enterprises for want of data on private enterprises. One does not know how inclusion of a private sector company like Reliance Industries Limited might affect the results obtained here. Further, as we have already pointed out, differences in efficiency between firms do not directly translate into differences in managerial efficiencies in the absence of proper accounting for environmental differences between enterprises.[20] Thus efficiency in not only difficult to achieve, it is also tricky to measure.

---

[20] This point is most relevant in comparing efficiencies between the Numaligarh Refinery and other companies, as we will see in Chapter 7.

Chapter 5

Estimation of Technical Efficiency Using Stochastic Frontier

"I don't doubt that it (R&D) is the largest ultimate source. But there seems to be a lot of productivity improvement that originates in people and processes that are not usually connected with R&D. Some of it comes form the shop floor, form the ideas of experienced and observant production workers."

Solow, R.M. (2001)

Introduction

One way to approach the task of measuring efficiency in a multifaceted real work environment is to put the whole problem in an abstract setting. We have discussed the concept of efficiency along with its limitations in the previous chapter. Now we come to the question of its estimation using Stochastic Frontier Analysis (SFA). The basic idea is that fully efficient operation gives the highest feasible level of product from a given set of resources. This gives the idea of an abstract production frontier, introduced in the last chapter, that can be characterized as:

$$Y = F(K, L),\ \ F_K, F_L > 0, F_{KK}, F_{LL} < 0$$

Use of this simple form involves heroic assumptions. Apart from the assumptions on marginal productivity what is involved is use of single indices of *Y, L* and *K* for essentially heterogeneous entities. However, the marginal conditions are not directly used in the estimation process other than their influence in the choice of the form of the production function.

The notion of technical efficiency is derived from this abstraction in the form of a production function.[1] As we have discussed in the last chapter, a producer is said to be technically inefficient unless he operates on the

---

[1] We draw heavily on Coelli, Rao and Battise (1998) and Kumbhakar and Lovell (2000) to summarize the literature that forms the basis of our analysis of efficiency.

frontier. This notion is silent about the choice of factor combination. If there is substitutability among productive factors the combination in which they are used in production should depend on relative prices. So, there is a question of efficient choice of factor combinations. Here comes the notion of input allocative efficiency.[2] Unless a producer is fully efficient following both the above notions he is incurring some cost due to inefficiency.

At another level of abstraction, the cost frontier, which is the dual of the production frontier, is capable of taking into account loss of efficiency due to both the possible failures—technical and allocative. In fact, cost efficiency (CE), or overall economic efficiency, can be viewed as the product of (input-based) technical efficiency (TE) and input allocative efficiency (AE) [Farrel, 1957]. Obviously, CE is a more comprehensive measure. Its estimation requires data on total expenditure, input prices and output quantity indices. Provided data are available, estimation of CE has often been preferred to that of output based TE. Further, theoretically it is possible to decompose CE into input-based TE[3] and AE. For this purpose input quantity data or input cost shares are needed. But, apart from the severe data requirements, this separation is technically challenging as, in this case, CE is to be estimated along with production technology and then decomposed into input-based TE and AE. Efficiency of estimates of CE further requires that prices should vary across firms, which is a requirement often not satisfied [Coelli, *et al.,* 1998; p. 211]. These considerations, compounded by severe data

---

[2] The relevance of the concept of allocative efficiency, though theoretically very nice and interesting, in the context of petroleum refineries is not very clear. We have discussed in Chapter 1 that no two refineries are identical. Though all the refineries refine crude oil (not of identical quality), the products are not identical. Plant design and factor requirements vary according to differences in thrusts in production and once a plant is set up there is very little scope of factor substitution. And, for all practical purposes, petroleum crude is the only material input—giving little scope for substitution between material inputs.

[3] The two measures of TE are identical if production technology shows constant returns to scale or if production is fully efficient. Otherwise, input-based TE is greater than output-based TE when returns to scale is increasing and *vice versa* (Kumbhakar and Lovell, 2000).

constraints, lead to confine ourselves in Chapter 7 to the estimation of output-based TE.[4] So, we discuss only the related models briefly. Interested readers may follow the references for detailed discussion of all the relevant issues.

5.1 Production Frontier Models

Deterministic production frontier models (corrected ordinary least squares, COLS, and modified ordinary least squares, MOLS) have the underlying assumption that technical efficiency varies across firms in a way independent of the observed explanatory variables; randomly in that sense. Let us assume that cross-sectional data on the quantities of "N" inputs (with only two factors, K and L, $N = 2$) used to produce a single product are available for each of "I" producers. A production frontier model can be written as:

$$Y_i = F\,(X_i - \beta).TE_i \qquad ...(5.1)$$

Here TE_i is defined as $Y_i \,/\, F\,(X_i, \beta)$, which implies that Y_i achieves its maximum feasible value $F\,(X_i, \beta)$ if and only if $TE_i = 1$. Otherwise, $TE_i\,(< 1)$ provides a measure of the shortfall.

Stochastic production frontier models take into account producer specific random shocks. So, shortfall in observed output from maximum feasible value for the given quantity of inputs (X_i) is caused not only by technical inefficiency but also by random shock caused by influences not accounted for and even beyond control. We introduce what is called a white noise (ν) term, i.e., a normally, independently and identically distributed random variable with zero mean, to account for what is left out of account in the production function. This noise is supposed to be capable of affecting output both favourably or unfavourably. We write:

---

[4] Bandunenko, *et al.* (2006) has suggested measurement of AE without using price data. They propose a measure of AE based on the output-oriented distance to the frontier in a profit-technicl efficiency space which does not require information on input prices. The traditional approach based on input prices, which are rarely known at the firm level, is then compared with the new approach using a Monte-Carlo experiment. High correlation is observed.

$$Y_i = F(X_i, \beta)\exp(v_i)TE_i$$

Maximum feasible output for the producer '*i*' is $F(X_i, \beta)\exp(v_i)$.

So, $TE_i = Y_i / F(X_i - \beta).\exp(v_i)$. Let us write $TE_i = \exp(-u_i)$. Since $TE_i \le 1, u_i \ge 0$, i.e., this error is one-sided. The two-sided random production shocks are left out of consideration in the relatively simple deterministic models. In that case we can write (5.1) as:

$$Y_i = F(X_i, \beta)\exp(-u_i) \qquad ...(5.2)$$

Assuming $F(X_i, \beta)$ to take Cobb-Douglas form, the deterministic production frontier model, which does not consider production shocks, takes the form:

$$\ln Y_i = \beta_0 + \sum_n \beta_n \ln X_{ni} - u_i \qquad ...(5.3)$$

(5.3) is a linear regression model with non-positive disturbances. The objective is to obtain estimates of β_n which describes the structure of the production frontier and also to obtain estimates[5] of u_i so that we can find $TE_i = \exp(-u_i)$. Whatever estimation methodology is used, it must incorporate the restriction on the error term.

In his discussion of Farrell's (1957) original paper, Winsten (1957) suggested that (5.3) could be estimated in two steps. The first step is OLS which gives consistent estimates of β_n. OLS estimates are also unbiased for slope parameters, but not for β_0. Since the estimated errors have mean zero while the restriction is that $u_i \ge 0$, it is suggested that the estimated intercept term $\hat{\beta}_0$ (the symbol "^" over a variable being used to denote the estimated value) be shifted up ("corrected") to ensure that the estimated frontier bounds the data from above. So, COLS intercept is suggested to be:

[5] Clearly, for the representation of $TE_i = \exp(-u_i)$, u_i has a very convenient interpretation of being the approximate measure of subtractive inefficiency from logarithm of output when inefficiency is not very large.

$$\hat{\beta}_0^* = \hat{\beta}_0 + \max(\hat{u}) \qquad ...(5.4)$$

[note that $\hat{u}_i$'s are OLS estimates of (–) u_i]

Then the COLS errors are

$$(-)\hat{u}_i^* = \hat{u}_i - \max(\hat{u}) \qquad ...(5.5)$$

The maximum being taken over all *i*'s. It is ensured that $\hat{u}_i^* \geq 0$ as $\max(\hat{u}) > 0$. At least one $\hat{u}_i^* = 0$. Then we can have

$$TE_i = \exp(-\hat{u}_i^*) \qquad ...(5.6)$$

(5.6) gives consistent estimates of the term *TE* in (5.1). However, to call the term technical efficiency we implicitly assume without providing any justification that efficiency is distributed in a way that serves our well-known needs for OLS.

Also, the simplistic "correction" for biased estimate of β_0 by OLS, as suggested by COLS implies that the 'best practice' production technology is parallel to, i.e., of the same structure as, the estimated 'central tendency' production technology. This is unnecessarily restrictive and means that COLS frontier does not necessarily bound the data from above as closely as possible. Afriat (1972) and Richmond (1974) proposed an interesting variation on COLS. They suggested that OLS disturbance of the deterministic model (5.3) may be reasonably assumed to follow an explicit one-sided distribution like the half-normal or exponential. The idea is that increasing degrees of inefficiencies should be increasingly unlikely. This idea has been implemented in a theoretically more satisfying way in stochastic frontier models later. But they suggested a modification of the COLS procedure under which the biased estimate of β_0 is shifted up by the mean of the assumed one-sided distribution. So,

$$\hat{\beta}_i^{**} = \hat{\beta}_0 + E(\hat{u}_i') \qquad ...(5.7)$$

sided error due to inefficiency become important. Distribution of the random disturbance is standard in econometrics, but that of the one-sided error is open to question. Several alternatives have been suggested; these are half-normal, exponential, truncated normal and gamma distributions. Thus we have a choice of a combination of assumptions; the standard normal distribution of the random disturbance term (v) and one for the distribution of the one-sided random variable (u). Under the assumption of either normal or exponential distribution for u, the imposition is that the modal value of inefficiency in zero while truncated normal or gamma distributions give the choice of the modal value on the basis of observations. The cost of this flexibility is the burden on data to estimate an additional parameter – the modal value. The flexibility is generally preferred. This preference along with ready accessibility to software often leads to the choice of the normal-truncated normal model which we also have adopted for our present study. We discuss the particular model below. An important point to note here, as already indicated in the previous chapter, is that monte carlo studies have shown the choice of the distribution for the one-sided error to affect the estimates of inefficiency but, generally, not such that the ranking of firms by inefficiency or the composition of the top and bottom deciles by efficiency scores is substantially altered.

5.3 Maximum Likelihood Estimation: The Normal-Truncated Normal Model

It was introduced by Stevenson (1980). The model given in (5.9) is further specified as:

a) v_i's are independently and identically distributed (IID) as $N(0, \sigma_v^2)$; this is a standard assumption regarding random disturbances.

b) Thus u_i's are *IID* $N^+(\mu, \sigma_u^2)$. Thus $u \geq 0$ is truncated below at zero, but the distribution is allowed to have a non-zero mode. The idea is that a low level of inefficiency is very common but beyond the modal level of inefficiency increasing inefficiency is increasingly unlikely. It allows the modal level to be estimated from observations. This model is often preferred because of this flexibility.

c) v_i and u_i are distributed independently of each other and, also, of the regressors.

The truncated density function is given by

$$f(u) = \frac{1}{\sqrt{2\pi}.\sigma_u \Phi\left(\mu/\sigma_u\right)} e^{\frac{-(u-\mu)^2}{2\sigma_u^2}} \qquad (5.10)$$

where μ is the mode of the normal distribution truncated below at zero and $\Phi(\cdot)$ is the standard normal cumulative distribution function. (5.10) collapses to the half-normal density when $\mu = 0$.

Now, the joint density function of u and v is the product of their individual density functions. Then by substituting for v using the relation $\varepsilon_i = v_i - u_i$ we can obtain the joint density of u and ε. Hence, we get the marginal density function of ε by integrating over the whole range of u. In the case of normal-truncated normal model, it has been derived from the joint density function of v and u under the above mentioned assumptions that the marginal density function of ε is:

$$f(\varepsilon) = \int_0^\infty f(\varepsilon, u)du = \frac{1}{\sigma}\phi\left(\frac{\varepsilon+\mu}{\sigma}\right)\Phi\left(\frac{\mu}{\sigma\lambda} - \frac{\varepsilon\lambda}{\sigma}\right)\left[\Phi\left(\frac{\mu}{\sigma_u}\right)\right]^{-1} \quad ...(5.11)$$

$f(\varepsilon)$ is asymmetrically distributed with mean and variance

$$E(\varepsilon) = -E(u) = -\frac{\mu a}{2} - \frac{\sigma_u a}{\sqrt{2\sigma_u}} e^{-\mu^2/2\sigma_u^2},$$

$$V(\varepsilon) = \mu^2 \frac{a}{2}\left(1 - a/2\right) + \frac{a}{2}\left(\frac{\pi - a}{\pi}\right)\sigma_u^2 + \sigma_v^2 \quad ...(5.12)$$

where $\sigma^2 = \sigma_u^2 + \sigma_v^2$ and $\lambda = \sigma_u/\sigma_v$; and $\phi(\cdot)$ is the standard normal density function and $a = \left[\Phi\left(\mu/\sigma_u\right)\right]^{-1}$. The parameterization from σ_u and σ_v to σ and λ is convenient. It is easy to see that $\lambda \to \infty$ when either $\sigma_u \to \infty$ or $\sigma_v \to 0$ which means that the one-sided error component supposed to be due to inefficiency dominates the symmetric error component due to random shock. The opposite case is one of only random error and no inefficiency; this takes us to the case of OLS estimation.

The Normal-Truncated Normal distribution has three parameters; one is placement parameter μ and the other two are spread parameters, σ_u and σ_v. These parameters are estimated along with the parameters of the production function. The log-likelihood function for estimation of the parameters of the production frontier along with those of the distribution functions of the errors can be estimated by using the maximum-likelihood method. For this purpose we need specification of the format of the production function. Transcendental logarithmic (trans-log) format is a generalized one, Cobb-Douglas format being a special case of the general format. So, the former is often preferred but the later still remains a favourite to econometricians. Statistical hypothesis testing is possible to check whether the generalized format gives a superior fit to the data or, if there exists significant one-sided error or inefficiency. These points will come into discussion in Chapter 7 where we will take up our actual estimation.

Our present concern is determination of individual producer specific inefficiency. We may not here that technical efficiency of the ith firm is $TE_i = e^{-u_i}$. However, u_i is not observable. Even if the true values of the parameters of the production function (β) were known, only the difference $\varepsilon_i = v_i - u_i$ could be observed. The best predictor of u_i is the conditional expectation of u_i given the value of $\varepsilon_i = v_i - u_i$ (Jondrow *et al.*, referred to as JLMS, 1982).

It has been shown that the conditional distribution $f(u/\varepsilon)$ is given as:

$$f(u \mid \varepsilon) = \frac{f(u,\varepsilon)}{f(\varepsilon)} = \frac{1}{\sqrt{2\pi}\sigma_* \left[1 - \Phi\left(-\tilde{\mu}/\sigma_*\right)\right]} e^{-\frac{(u-\tilde{\mu})^2}{2\sigma_*^2}} \quad \text{...(5.13)}$$

$f(u_i | \varepsilon_i)$ is distributed as $N^+(\tilde{\mu}_i, \sigma_*^2)$, where, $\tilde{\mu} = (-\sigma_u^2 \varepsilon_i + \mu\sigma_v^2)/\sigma^2$

and $\sigma_*^2 = \dfrac{\sigma_u^2 \sigma_v^2}{\sigma^2}$.

Thus either mean or mode of the conditional distribution can be used to estimate the technical efficiency of each producer, $TE_i = (e^{-\tilde{u}_i})$; $\tilde{u}_i$ is obtained from

$$E(u_i | \varepsilon_i) = \sigma_* \left[\frac{\tilde{\mu}_i}{\sigma_*} + \frac{\phi(\tilde{\mu}_i / \sigma_*)}{[1 - \Phi(-\tilde{\mu}_i / \sigma_*)]} \right] \text{; or,}$$

$$M(u_i | \varepsilon_i) = \begin{cases} \tilde{\mu}_i & \text{if } \tilde{\mu}_i \geq 0 \\ 0 & \text{otherwise} \end{cases} \quad \text{... (5.14)}$$

Alternatively, $$TE_i = E(e^{\{-u_i\}} | \varepsilon_i) = \frac{1 - \Phi\left[\sigma_* - \tilde{u}_i / \sigma_*\right]}{1 - \Phi\left(\tilde{u}_i / \sigma_*\right)} . e^{\left\{-\tilde{u}_i + \frac{\sigma_*^2}{2}\right\}} \quad \text{...(5.15)}$$

This estimator is unbiased but inconsistent. Technical efficiency predictor computed in the Frontier (Coelli, 1996) programme that we use in the present study is obtained from (5.15) by using the maximum likelihood estimates of the unknown parameters.

Battese and Coelli (1992) proposed a model for time varying technical inefficiency for stochastic frontier approach with panel data. Technical inefficiency effects are defined by

$$u_{it} = [e^{-\eta(t-T)}]u_i, \quad i = 1, 2, \ldots N;\ t = 1, 2, \ldots T; \quad \text{...(5.16)}$$

Where u_i's are assumed to be IID truncated normal random variables as defined above and η is an unknown scalar to be estimated. Clearly, in this formulation $u_{iT} = u_i$, which is the technical inefficiency of the ith firm in the last period. For other periods, it can be calculated from (5.16). Another obvious implication of this innovative application is that the ranking of firms do not change over time. Thus, when firms improve or deteriorate in efficiency unevenly, as one would normally expect, so as to impact their ranking, the method given by (5.16) is unable to reflect the change properly. Further, the case where all the firms improve in efficiency uniformly one may be perplexed to explain it unless there is some clear change in atmosphere like change in government policy. Otherwise the situation may be indistinguishable from technical change as discussed in the previous chapter.

5.4 Some Empirical Applications for the Indian Economy

Page, J. M. (1984) applied deterministic production frontier approach to study the relative levels of technical efficiency in four Indian industries. Using cross-section data a trans-log production function relating four factor inputs to total output was fit to the survey data. He used linear programming technique to minimize the sum of the deviations from the frontier, subject to the constraint that all observations lay on or below it. The resulting deterministic frontier, as there is no allowance for any stochastic shock, ascribes all variations from predicted best practice output to technical inefficiency. "Each firm is assigned an efficiency index equal to the ratio of its actual to predicted output, ... which may be found as the antilog of the slack variable in the programming problem. The value of the index provides a measure of relative technical efficiency." He focused on the association between TE and firm size and concluded that there existed little systematic relationship between firm size and technical efficiency.

Battese and Coelli (1992) applied the stochastic frontier approach to study efficiency of paddy farming in India. They used panel data collected from a particular village to estimate time-varying efficiency and observed a rising trend of efficiency. Fifteen farmers were observed for ten years. A total of 129 observations were used, so 21 observations were missing from the panel. The stochastic frontier production function was defined by:

$$\log (Y) = \beta_0 + \beta_1 \log (\text{Land}) + \beta_2 (\text{Land ratio, Irrigated/unirrigated}) + \beta_3 \log (\text{Labour}) + \beta_4 \log (\text{Bulloek}) + \beta_5 \log (\text{costs}) + v - u,$$

Each variable takes subscripts to refer to the ith farmer and the tth observation.

The frontier function is estimated for five basic models:

Model 1.0 involves all parameters being estimated;

Model 1.1 assumes that $\mu = 0$;

Model 1.2 assumes that : $\quad = 0$;

Model 1.3 assumes that $\mu = \quad = 0$; and

Model 1.4 assumes that $\quad = \mu = \quad = 0$.

Tests of hypotheses involving the parameters of the distribution of the u_i-random variables (farm effects) are obtained by using the generalized likelihood-ratio statistic. Several hypotheses were considered for different distributional assumptions. Given the specifications of the stochastic frontier with time-varying farm effects (Model 1.0), they concluded that the traditional average production function (Model 1.4) was not an adequate representation of the data. Further, the hypotheses that time-invariant models for farm effects apply were also rejected.

However, the hypothesis that the half-normal distribution is an adequate representation for the distribution of the farm effects (Moles 1.1) was not rejected. Given that the half-normal distribution is assumed appropriate to define the distribution of the farm effects, the hypothesis that the yearly farm effects are time invariant was also rejected by the data. Given the specifications of Model 1.1 (involving the half-normal distribution), the technical efficiencies of the individual paddy farmers were calculated.

Neogi and Ghosh (1994) studied technical efficiency of Indian manufacturing industries for the period 1974-75 to 1987-88. They have used both the deterministic and stochastic frontier approaches. COLS method showed an overall declining trend across industries. Use of a time-varying (fixed ranking) stochastic frontier models confirmed the decreasing efficiency of Indian industries over the period concerned. Interestingly, the study also sought to distinguish between technical efficiency effects and technical change by incorporating a time variable in the production function and found significant presence of both the effects in the relevant sector of the economy.

De (2004) estimated technical efficiency using the stochastic frontier approach for the Indian banking sector. His uses generalized least squares following Cornwell, Schmidt and Sickles (1990) to estimate time varying technical efficiency. This approach avoids the distributional assumptions necessary to disentangle random noise from the one-sided variable representing technical efficiency. However, the cost of this freedom in the burden of estimation of a huge number of parameters as one can see from the model used:

$$\ln Y_{it} = \theta_{i1} + \theta_{i2}t + \theta_{i3}t^2 + \sum_n \beta_n \ln X_{nit} + v_{it} \qquad ...(5.\ 17)$$

Required number of parameters to be estimated in this case is 3I + N + 1 (including an intercept). Efficiency of estimates become questionable unless the panel is very long.

De used panel data covering period 1985-96 for eighteen banks. He avoids trans-log production function as "trans-log production function does not satisfy the regularity conditions and is found to be not well behaved for banking industry in India ..." So, a Cobb-Douglas technology was applied using four inputs and two alternative measures of output. TE for the industry as a whole was found to be time-invariant, i.e., unresponsive to liberalization policy. Also, the findings were not unambiguous regarding relative efficiency of public sector and private sector (Indian ownership) banks. However, foreign banks showed the highest levels of efficiency.

Kumbhakar and Sarkar (2005) estimated cost efficiency of public and private sector banks in India over the period 1986 to 2000. The study illustrates how the stochastic frontier approach could be used to explain the variation in efficiency in terms of exogenous factors that could be of use to policy makers. The findings of the study indicate that inefficiency tended to decline over time that coincides with the liberalization of the banking sector. Another interesting finding of the study is that private banks were in general more efficient compared to the public sector banks in India.

Datta (2008) studied technical efficiency trend of public sector oil refining companies. The approach taken in the study is maximum likelihood estimation as we have discussed above and the subject of the study is the same as our study presented in Chapter 7. What differs is only time coverage. Datta (2008) considered a fourteen-year period, 1991–92 to 2004-05. There were five public sector companies that operated over the entire period. One new company, NRL, started operation in 2000. Both trans-log and Cobb-Douglas forms of production function were tried in eight regressions covering different sets of data. It is interesting to note that statistical hypothesis testing could not establish superiority of the trans-log form over the relatively simple Cobb-Douglas form. The study could detect only a weak evidence of a rising trend of technical efficiency over the last five years – 2000–01 to 2004–05 when NRL was included in the study. The finding is particularly interesting, though five-years is too short a period, as the period relates to the new liberalized regime in the administration of public sector oil refineries. Interestingly, NRL was found to be the least efficient company in the set. No such trend was found either over the whole period of fourteen years or over the first nine years. Neither was the rising efficiency observable when NRL was excluded from the panel reducing the total number of observations in the panel from 30 to 25.

In view of the importance of petroleum for a modern economy, petroleum refining got a prominent place in the government's scheme of building up of public sector industries after Independence. In terms of turnover, the oil refining public sector companies (PSCs) together constitute by far the largest public sector industry in India today. Naturally, the performance of the PSCs draws a lot of public interest. It is of great academic as well as economic interest, therefore, whether the weak evidence of rising trend is maintained with data for four more years, giving 24 new observations, being available now. This issue will be taken up in Chapter 7.

Chapter 6

Measurement of Variables

Great advances have been made in theory and in econometric techniques, but these will be wasted unless they are applied to the right data.

Zvi Griliches, 1994

Indroduction

In Chapter 1 we have noted that each modern refinery consists of several interconnected units but two refineries may not have identical sets of units. They normally do not refine the same types of crude in identical composition. Naturally, this should have some reflection somewhere on the refining process. While these differences in detail should be kept in view, it is nevertheless true that different refineries produce broadly similar products. One great challenge with econometric modeling is that in order to keep the model reasonably simple and intuitively appealing we need single indices of heterogeneous entities classified as the product and primary inputs—labour and capital. Very often, as in the case of oil refineries, these indices are not readily available from published data. So, the researcher has to find ways of obtaining the indices. We discuss below how we arrived at our estimates of the variables relevant for our purpose.

6.1 Capital

One argument in the production function is capital which is most often taken as capital stock. The concept[1] of capital is rather vague and, therefore, its estimation is a very tricky issue. But somehow we suppose we know what it is and proceed to estimate it. That does not make it very easy but life goes on. In the present case no ready estimate of capital stock suitable for use in analysis of the production function does exist. The estimates of fixed assets (or gross block) given by annual reports of

[1] This refers to the Cambridge controversy. See Garegnani, 1971, and the related references.

companies are calculated at historical prices; these are neither at current nor at constant prices. However, changes in gross block are always at current prices because of the historical-price accounting. These changes give direct and more reliable information on capital *formation* than figures on investment in fixed capital, because investments take some time to be transformed into capital stock ready for use, which is measured as gross block. Using changes in gross block it is possible to arrive at an estimate of capital stock at constant prices. We have, however, estimated indices of what we have called "service capital" following the method suggested by Datta (2006).

Service capital is the appropriate argument in the production function because the value of capital stock is affected by the longevity of different elements in the stock but capital service which is supposed to be the relevant input in production in real time should depend on the efficiency of the stock, not its longevity. Let us explain in brief. Suppose the market value of an item of capital to be determined by the service that can be derived from the item in production. Suppose two such items of the same market value are a machine that lasts for 20 years and a computer that lasts for 5 years; so, the value of capital stock is 2 times the value of the machine. Also assume for simplicity, as in the case of One-Hoss-Shay Method (OHSM) of estimation, that physical depreciation does not affect the efficiency of machines and so, services derived from them. Then after one year of use the machine has 19 years (i.e., 95%) of service still left and the computer has 4 years (i.e., 80%) of service. Then, abstracting from discounting for the future, the value to the capital stock at the end of one year will be 1.75 times the value of the new machine. But they render the same service in the second year as in the first year. So, capital input in production is really not affected though the value of the stock is affected. Thus, the value of capital stock is not the right argument in the production function. This consideration leads us to use an index of service capital. Before going into its actual measurement it should be pertinent to explain in brief the issues involved.

The method used by the Central Statistical Organization (CSO) of India in its measurement of capital stock is the one recommended by the UN System of National Accounts (S.N.A., 1993) — the perpetual inventory method (PIM). The PIM involves finding figures for lifetime of different types of capital goods, computing price indices for these goods, estimating gross fixed capital formation by type of assets and adopting a formula for depreciation of the value of capital goods. Value of machines and structures depreciate due to aging, which reduces the remaining productive life as well as efficiency of assets. Though aging need not necessarily affect the productivity of fixed assets in every passing period that may be important for efficiency of assets particularly in the advanced stages of their lives. The decline in the value of fixed assets in the course of production, because of decline in efficiency as well as the fact that the asset has passed part of its fruitful life is treated as capital consumption or depreciation.

A crucial question for the estimation of capital stock is how we should determine the formula for the measurement of depreciation. As per usual practice, and the method adopted by the CSO of India, it is based on the assumption of a uniform rate of loss of value over a fixed lifetime of assets. Clearly, the problem involves an estimation of lifetime of different types of machines and structures. The assumed lifetime can at best be a rough approximation supposed to be validated by the law of large numbers.[2] Thus the assumption of a fixed lifetime can be justified only as an average. Life can be stretched and the decision to discard a machine is related to either rising maintenance cost or obsolescence.[3] Estimation of lifetime involves foresight of the possibilities. Once the lifetime is determined the question is what path describes the wearing process of the asset over its lifetime. Resolution of this question is no less difficult than finding the lifetime itself. But let us pause and think – if the objective is to track the path of efficiency of capital goods because that is what determines the service it can render, then for determining the relevant argument of the production function it should be more appropriate to talk of the age-efficiency (A-E) profile instead of the depreciation (of value) profile.

---

[2] The law of large numbers does not help when we consider a small unit with a limited number of machines. In that case replacement cost can be lumpy, not uniform. The idea behind using a uniform rate of depreciation comes from the following consideration: let a depreciation fund (inventory) be created. There exists some uniform rate of accumulation in the fund such that in the long run it is just sufficient to meet the requirements for replacement of machines as and when required (Scott, M., 1984).

[3] Henderson and Quandt (1980), Ch-12.

6.2 Implications of Two Approaches: PIM and OHSM

The PIM

Datta (2006) establishes that PIM with a linear depreciation profile (PIMLD) implies that the net revenue (*m(t)*) earned in time '*t*' from capital goods declines linearly by an amount determined by the relevant rate of discount (ρ), life-time (T) of capital goods and the present value of the stock at the beginning of life (A_0). Thus, assuming efficiency of a machine to be proportional to the net revenue earned by the machine which can, therefore, be taken as an index of efficiency of capital stock, *m(t)* can be taken as equivalent to the A-E profile. The A-E profile implied by the PIMLD is a straight line. It can be shown that the relations may be written in the form of equations (6.1) and (6.2).

$$m(t) = \rho A_0\left(1-\frac{t}{T}+\frac{1}{\rho T}\right) = \rho A_t + A_0/T \quad \text{...(6.1)}$$

and $$m'(t) = -\rho\frac{A_0}{T}(<0) = -\rho m(T) \quad \text{...(6.2)}$$

From (6.1), $m(0) = \rho A_0\left(1+\frac{1}{\rho T}\right) = (\rho T+1)\frac{A_0}{T}$

and $$m(T) = \rho A_0\frac{1}{\rho T} = \frac{A_0}{T} \quad \text{...(6.1a)}$$

Thus the A-E profile implied by the PIMLD is a straight line. Clearly, a constant and negative change per unit time implies an increasing proportional rate of decline in returns. Further, (1a) shows that the terminal efficiency is also a function of the life-time.

For $\rho = 0.1$ and $T = 20$, $m(0) = 3\,m(\text{T})$.

For $A_0 = 100$, $m(0) = 15$ and $m(T) = 5$

But, for $T = 10$ and $\rho = 0.1$ we would have, for the same A_0, $m(0) = 20$ and $m(T) = 10$.

Thus, given the rate of discount and the lifetime itself, PIMLD gives the formula for the uniform decline in efficiency of capital goods over their lifetime. This does not seem to be a very comfortable representation of the reality. One may argue that steady and linear decline in efficiency is a very restrictive case. Repair and maintenance may be viewed to maintain the efficiency of capital goods intact for a considerable period though more frequent stoppages and rise in maintenance cost as machines get old may lead to their replacement. Alternatively, machines may be replaced due to obsolescence even though operational efficiency remains high (Henderson and Quandt, 1980, ch.12).[4] An electric bulb may be an extreme example (its illumination remaining rather constant

---

[4] A concrete example should be interesting here. Numaligarh Refinery in Assam was set up at a cost of Rs. 2.5 thousand crores. The cost of plant and machinery is roughly 1.5 thousand crores. The rest is cost of civil engineering works (including the cost of the township), royalty and know-how expenses, process design and supervision charges etc. The refinery has a number of sub-systems like the crude and vacuum distillation units, delayed coker unit, hydrockracker unit, hydrogen unit, etc. Each of the above entioned units uses a number of equipments like columns and column internals, heat exchangers, air cooled exchangers, pumps and drives, compressors, etc. The problem of decay, breakdown and obsolescence concern mainly these equipments constituting 60% of the project cost. Every year the plant is overhauled and every alternate year the overhauling is extra-intensive. During overhauling the plant is shut down for a fortnight or so. Even then need for unscheduled maintenance arises during operation of plants. Replacements of parts are treated as current cost so long as these are minor and keep productive capacity un-enhanced. According to senior engineers, the plant is expected to operate at the peak of its efficiency without really major replacements of equipments for a period of 100,000 hours or 12 years when operated for 24 hours a day and 350 days per annum, only if regular maintenance (and overhauling) is done. Thus for 12 years the plant is expected to yield roughly constant net revenue. After this period replacement of equipments will become part of a regular process. It is pertinent to note here that a unit normally goes on working at full efficiency for many years beyond the life-time even though 95% of its historic cost (the rest is treated as junk value) is wiped off the book of accounts as depreciation. There are several refineries with age of units several times their prescribed lifetimes. These are represented in the gross-block figures cited in books of accounts only to the extent of 5% of their historic cost. This is meaningful only because a plant is continuously renewed – not discarded altogether.

until it suddenly gets fused, so efficiency does not fall), but it is a case worth pursuing. This brings us to the consideration of the one-hoss-shay method (OHSM) of estimation of capital stock. But, at this stage we should emphasize that if we can ignore the finer issues regarding the rate of decline in net revenue for each period, the PIMLD may be considered passable as a measure of the real asset value of capital stock or what the US Bureau of Labour Statistics calls 'wealth' stock. For an estimate of service capital what is important is productivity or efficiency of the capital good during the period concerned, not the present asset value.

The One-Hoss-Shay Method (OHSM)

The OHSM considers depreciation to be zero until the end of the assumed lifetime when the capital good is supposed to be junked. Clearly, the approach is not concerned with asset value of capital stock. The OHSM seems to be appropriate for measuring aggregate capital stock when the capital stock is taken to represent productive capacity or potential capital services if the assumption that the productive capacity remains unchanged over the lifetime of the capital goods can be justified. Capital stock is computed under this method as follows:

Let I_t = gross investment at 't', K_t = aggregate gross capital stock at 't' defined as:

$$K_t = \int_{(t-T)}^{t} I_s ds \quad \text{[We assume lifetime of capital goods} = T\text{]}$$

So, $$K_T = \int_0^T I_0 e^{rt} dt = (I_0 / r)[e^{rt}]_0^T$$

[Let uniform rate of growth of gross investment = r]

$$= (I_0 / r)(e^{rT} - 1) = I_0 / \mu \text{ (say)} \qquad ...(6.3)$$

So, $$\mu = I_0 / K_T = \frac{r}{(e^{rT} - 1)} \qquad ...(6.4)$$

Equation (6.4) gives the intuition that μ is the rate of depreciation. This should be clear if we consider the analogy of aggregate capital stock in discrete time. Capital stock K_T (at the beginning of the period) is net of expired capital (of period prior to '0'). Investment (gross) of period 't' is operative as capital from $(t + 1)$ onwards. So, I_0 starts operating in '1' and works up to 'T'. It expires in the beginning of '$T + 1$'.

So, using (6.3), $K_{T+1} = \sum_{1}^{T} I_t = (K_T + I_T - I_0) = (1-\mu)K_T + I_T$ ....(6.5)

Equation (6.5) gives μ the interpretation of an ***equivalent proportional rate of depreciation***[5] (EPD) under OHSM when gross investment grows exponentially at the rate 'r'. We will take up the point again later. What follows from the above discussion is that under the assumption of a uniform exponential rate of growth (r) of investment there exists an EPD for the computation of GFCS under the OHSM. This EPD is given by

$$\mu = \frac{r}{(e^{rT} - 1)}.$$

6.3 EPD under the PIM

We can proceed to find the EPD for the PIMLD under the assumption of constant exponential rate of growth of investment and then compare this with the EPD under the OHSM. PIMLD assumes a uniform time rate of decay of capital. Thus an investment I_t in time 't' (end of the period) that becomes operative at the beginning of '$t + 1$', lives up to '$t + T$'. In '$t + T$' the value of the investment reduces to just $(^1/_T)$th of that of a brand new machine before the value reduces to zero in the next period and the machine expires.

Thus what remains of I_t at the beginning of 'T' is $I_t(1-\delta(T-1-t))$, where δ is the rate of decay. So, net capital stock at $(T+1)$ (beginning of the period) is:

---

[5] Here a more appropriate term is 'discard'. Depreciation is not considered at all as decline in the value of assets with aging is not taken into account. We gloss over the distinction between the two concepts.

$$K_{T+1} = I_0(1-\delta T) + I_1(1-\delta \overline{T-1}) + ...+ I_T(1-\delta \overline{T-T}).$$

[We denote by κ the value of capital stock by PIM in the beginning of '*T*'.]

When lifetime is '*T*' periods, $\delta = 1/T$; as is assumed in PIMLD, and we need not consider investment before I_0 as they have already expired. In fact, I_0 has also expired.

$$\text{So, } \kappa_{T+1} = \sum_1^T I_t - \delta \sum_1^T (T-t) I_t$$

$$= \sum_1^T I_t - \delta T \sum_1^T I_t + \delta \sum_1^T t.I_t = \delta \sum_1^T tI_t \qquad ...(6.6)$$

In continuous time we consider time increments of '*dt*' instead of 1. So,

we can write (6.6) as: $$\kappa_T = \delta \int_0^T tI_t dt$$

$$= I_0 \delta \int_0^T te^{rt} dt = I_0 \, \delta/r \int_0^T t.re^{rt} dt \quad \text{[Putting } I_t = I_0 e^{rt}\text{]}$$

$$= \frac{I_0}{r}\left(e^{rT} - 1/rT(e^{rT} - 1)\right). \quad \text{[putting } \delta = \frac{1}{T}\text{]} \qquad ...(6.7)$$

$$\text{or, } \quad I_0/\kappa_T = \frac{r}{e^{rT} - 1/rT(e^{rT} - 1)} = \nu \quad \text{(constant)} \qquad ...(6.8)$$

Comparing the ratio of investment in '0' to capital stock in '*T*' for PIMLD and OHSM, ν and μ, it is clear that κ_T for PIMLD is less than K_T for OHSM as the latter takes the sum of undepreciated investment accumulating over '*T*' periods while PIM takes the depreciated sum.

Further, under PIMLD,

$$\kappa_{T+1} = \kappa_T - \delta\left(\sum_0^{T-1} I_t\right) + I_T = \kappa_T - \delta.K_T + I_T \qquad ...(6.9)$$

(See equation (6.5), K_T= gross capital stock at 'T' under OHSM.)

Again, $K_T = {}^{I_0}\!/_{\mu} = \kappa_T\, {}^{V}\!/_{\mu}$. (After substitution from equation 6.8)

So, $\kappa_{T+1} = \kappa_T\left(1 - {}^{V}\!/_{\mu T}\right) + I_T$ [Putting $\delta = {}^{1}\!/_{T}$] ...(6.10)

This gives us a convenient formula for computing κ_t using $D = {}^{V}\!/_{\mu T}$ as the equivalent proportional rate of depreciation (EPD). Thus, under the assumption of a uniform exponential rate of growth (r) of investment, there exists an EPD for the computation of NFCS under the PIMLD. This EPD is given by $D = {}^{V}\!/_{\mu T}$.

It is clear from equation (6.6) that efficiency of capital stock is not the objective of measurement for NFCS; it is the depreciation of value that is the principal focus. Here it should be noted that we have subtly shifted from a particular type of asset to NFCS that involves aggregation of assets created over time. The above discussion has introduced the basic idea of an EPD. If the EPD can be found in a way consistent with efficiency units of capital stock, rather than value units relevant for PIM, we can proceed to estimation of service capital which is nothing but an index of capital stock in efficiency units that can also be treated as an index of capital service. In the next section we take up the issue.

6.4 Measurement of Service Capital

We have already noted that PIMLD gives the wealth stock and OHSM can be taken as giving the service capital only in the special case when stocks do not decline in efficiency over the lifetime. But in general efficiency is supposed to decline over time. Some form of decline in efficiency can be easily taken into account in the EPD format. Here the principal question is what the path of decline would be. This is an area, as discussed above, where we have lack of information and agreement.[6] As a convenient case we will consider geometric decline.

As already pointed out, the implication of the PIMLD is that for any given rate of discount efficiency declines (linearly) at the end of lifetime by a factor determined by the lifetime itself. This is a result, not a considered assumption. Moving the other way round, if the factor of terminal efficiency is known (again, it is an area of uncertainty but some implicit assumption is made in any estimate) one can easily find out the geometric rate of decline, α, and use this rate to find the EPD for computation of service capita index, which focuses on the decline in efficiency with aging but not decline in value due to passing of useful years of service. It should be clear that the above assumptions are akin to the assumption of a particular A-E profile.

Let S denote service capital. Then we can write:

$$S_T = \int_0^T I_0 e^{rt-\alpha(T-t)} dt = \frac{I_0 e^{-\alpha T}}{r+\alpha}[e^{(r+\alpha)T} - 1] \qquad \text{...(6.11)}$$

[As investment at the point t has suffered decay for time *(T-t)*.]

Now, $S_{T+1} = (1-\alpha)S_T - I_0 e^{-\alpha T} + I_T$, after substituting from (6.11) we have,

$$S_{T+1} = S_T\left[1-\left(\alpha+\frac{r+\alpha}{e^{(r+\alpha)T}-1}\right)\right]+I_T \qquad \text{...(6.12)}$$

Let us write $d = \alpha + \dfrac{r+\alpha}{e^{(r+\alpha)T}-1}$. Clearly, d is the EPD for service capital.

Thus, an estimate of service capital index can be obtained by using the EPD approach [equations (6.11) and (6.12)] by making suitable

[6] Several paths have been suggested in the literature though it has been recognized that no path is fully satisfactory or suitable for all cases. Moreover, different paths often yield very close results (Harper, M.J., 1982, Blades, D., 2001).

assumptions regarding the A-E profile. The relevant rate of depreciation is given by *d*.

The discerning reader must have noted that in obtaining the estimate for a sector of the economy or even for an industry an aggregation problem is involved. In our aggregative analysis we have sidetracked the problem putting the whole burden on a suitable choice of implicit average lifetime *T*. The average *T* is higher than the lifetime of short-lived assets and vice versa for long-lived assets. This means that the depreciation rate used by EPD approach correspondingly under and over-states the true rates. This would go some way to compensate what the EPD approach ignores—the higher rental price of short-lived assets. While the higher contribution (rental prices) of short-lived assets to the service potential is ignored, the contribution of older assets of the same category to the aggregate is enhanced by application of a smaller depreciation rate (caused by use of a larger than expected T) to bring some balance. Clearly the EPD approach will not be able to capture properly changes in service potential in the short run in times of rapid changes in proportions of short and long-lived assets, but the approach would be more reliable so far as trend of the aggregate is concerned. This is the price of ease[7] of aggregative analysis.

We have presented above three different concepts of depreciation for the three concepts—gross, net and service capital. Gross stock (OHSM) takes into account only discards at the end of lifetime. Net stock (PIMLD) considers discards as well as the depreciation of value caused by decline in remaining lifetime and decline in efficiency due to aging. Service capital considers discards and decline in efficiency, not the decline in value caused by reduction in remaining lifetime. Clearly, gross stock is a special case of service capital—it is the case of constant efficiency.

Table 6.1 provides values of *d* for different values of *r* and for α derived on the assumption that efficiency of capital goods decline by a factor of ½ or ⅓ at the end of lifetime. Obviously, *d* can be derived on the basis of alternative assumptions and we can obtain estimates of service capital by

[7] The alternative would be to evaluate the service efficiency of individual items of capital stock and add up.

using equation (6.12). It is important to note (Table 6.1) that d is much less susceptible to changes in r than to changes in T or α. This highlights the importance of the last two variables and gives some comfort to researchers engaged in actual estimation that the assumption of a constant r may not be a great knot inasmuch as the implied error is small.

Table 6.1: EPD's for Service Capital Estimation (d) for Alternative Values of 'r', 'T', and Terminal Efficiency of Capital Goods.

	Terminal Efficiency = 1/2		
Lifetime (T)	*d (for r = 0.08)*	*d (for r = 0.05)*	*d (for r = 0.10)*
10	0.11258	0.12125	0.10748
15	0.06858	0.07596	0.06457
20	0.04753	0.05374	0.04443
25	0.03554	0.04072	0.03319
	Terminal Efficiency = 1/3		
10	0.14331	0.15037	0.13919
15	0.09034	0.09627	0.08716
20	0.06467	0.06959	0.06225
25	0.04980	0.05386	0.04799

Source: Computed from formula for '*d*' given in the text.

Estimation of Service Capital Index

We now implement formulae (6.11) and (6.12) to obtain estimates of service capital indices for the oil refining public sector companies. The only estimate of capital stock available for the companies are the estimates of fixed assets (or gross block) provided in the annual reports and reproduced in Public Enterprises Survey Report (Govt. of India). These figures are aggregates of stocks of different vintages at historical prices. Obviously, changes in gross block are at current prices. As the first step we use the implicit price deflator of Net Fixed Capital Stock for the Public Sector Registered Manufacturing obtained from CSO estimate to deflate changes in gross block.

Now we come to the crucial question of finding the average lifetime 'T'. In view of the existence of a great number of plants and equipments of varying longevities and character in a single refinery, it seems to be a Herculean task for any individual researcher. Fortunately we have an escape. The international standard is to take average lifetime of refinery capital stock to be 20 years (Gary and Handwerk, 2001, p. 361). We use this information with a little modification. We have taken the lifetime to be 22 years. This rather arbitrary extension of lifetime can be justified on the consideration that scarcity of capital and relatively cheap labour in India would lead to more intensive maintenance and longer life of equipments in the country. Then we have taken arbitrarily the terminal efficiency to be ⅔rd that of the new stock. Our consideration is that in a sophisticated plant with a complex network of machines efficiency in a part of the network cannot be allowed to fall greatly if the network is to function with reasonable efficiency. PIM assumes the efficiency to fall to a small fraction towards the end of the lifetime. This must be inappropriate for refineries though we do not have any precise information about what the terminal efficiency should be. Some arbitrariness seems inevitable. We have only made it explicit rather than keeping it implicit.

Table 6.2: Estimates of Service Capital Indices for Oil Refining PSCs*

Year	*CPCL*	*BPCL*	*HPCL*	*IOCL*	*KRL*	*NRL*
1991–92	96115	258866	281673	667708	69302	—
1992–93	106063	278255	304177	729317	68058	—
1993–94	120027	301600	333752	802377	73292	—
1994–95	148250	332573	367935	842485	102228	—
1994–96	165388	365621	392622	994150	101748	—
1996–97	162602	394822	430856	1153429	108148	—
1997–98	160932	472286	500485	1336623	111635	—
1998–99	155815	529002	548837	1580318	113925	—
1999–00	188068	627224	730487	1955748	166134	—
2000–01	182894	682325	758169	2155554	167588	161609
2001–02	182300	728142	804090	2239708	173281	163542
2002–03	188270	754207	816942	2446687	173814	156023
2003–04	272798	806098	836336	2495041	173158	153387
2004–05	323114	872365	870349	2599491	179320	157082
2005–06	322377	960429	901886	2731538	197934	156489
2006–07	307917	977105	969204	3220149	214160	169789
2007–08	312686	989165	1105752	3223256	224216	169841
2008–09	313238	1029780	1098502	3387749	256504	168667

Estimated using the sources: Public Enterprises Survey (GoI), Diferent Issues; National Accounts Statistics (CSO), 2009, 2005 and 2001(Back series).

* We do not normalize the indices. The unit of capital service is taken as the service rendered by a measured stock worth Rs. 1 crore in the base year.

Given the above assumptions we can find out α and d. Now, we can straight away use equation (6.11) to find service capital index from the 22nd year onwards from the initial year of observation putting changes in gross block ($\Delta K = I_T$) in the equation. Since we have data from 1979–80 we can find the indices thus for only nine years. In order to find service capital indices for 1999–2000 and earlier years we use equation (6.12). It is here that the assumption of constancy of r is important (see discussion above on sensitivity of d to r). Clearly, the further backward we move, the smaller number of observations we have and, so, the lesser is our assumed r based on actual observations. This puts a restriction on how far backward we can move. In our exercise we have moved backward by nine years. So, our first estimate lacks nine observations on ΔK which is substituted by the assumption of constant r. We have taken a median value of growth rate of ΔK (from the rates obtained for different sixteen-year periods over the first twenty-two observations) as the relevant value of r. The estimates are presented in Table 6.2.

The principal merit of the EPD approach used by us here is that it can be easily applied once we determine the average lifetime and terminal efficiency. In spite of its limitations discussed above, we consider the EPD approach to be a marked improvement over the alternative of estimating capital stock through ad hoc adjustments of book values that are normally available from company balance sheets.

6.5 Segregation of Refining and Marketing Operations

After the estimation of service capital at the company level our problem is to segregate capital required for refining from that for marketing operations. Since only three—IOCL, BPCL and HPCL—out of six companies under consideration take up marketing of their own products as well as the bulk of products of other companies, while the three other companies—CPCL, KRL and NRL—do not engage in any substantive direct marketing operation, relative efficiencies cannot be comparable unless we can somehow solve the segregation problem.

A great problem is that such segregated account is not available from company sources or from any published document. Fortunately some clue in the form of break-up of the capital stock by its nature is provided by the BPCL Annual Report (2002–03). For other companies even this clue is not available. We have applied the clue for IOC and HPCL as well by assuming that capital stock required for marketing operations by the three companies is proportional to their respective volumes of operation. BPCL Annual Report (2002–03, pp. 82–83) also tells us that the quantity sold by the company in 2002–03 was roughly 2.5 times its own production. This allows us to attempt at the necessary segregation on the basis of the proportionality assumption mentioned above. BPCL Annual Report gives the following break-up (Table 6.3) of gross-block for the year 2002–03.

Table 6.3: Fixed Assets of BPCL, 2002–03

Particulars	*% of GB (rounded)*
1. Land, etc.	4.5
2. Buildings and Railway sideways	18.0
3. Plant and Machinery	21.0
4. Tanks and Pipelines	19.0
5. Dispensing Pumps	4.5
6. LPG Cylinders, Allied equipments etc	33.0
Total	100.0

We take dispensing pumps as required only for retail sale. Buildings and Railway sideways (item 2), Tanks and Pipelines (item 4), and LPG cylinders etc (item 6) are, however, required even by non-marketing companies. Since BPCL sells 2.5 times its own production, we divide the assets of the last three categories in the proportion 1:1:1.5. The underlying idea is that had the company engaged in marketing its own product only, it would require these assets in almost equal quantities each for production and marketing. Another 1.5 times that quantity is required for marketing of products purchased by the company from others. Thus, percentages of the four types of assets required for refining operations *vis-à-vis* marketing operations may be taken as given in Table 6.4. While the above division is not based on any precise information, the exercise at least goes some way towards making a reasonable separation of assets.

It transpires from the above exercise that roughly 55% of the capital stock of BPCL in 2002–03 belonged to its marketing operation. We further note that BPCL sales was almost 60% higher than its own production in 1990–91 (Annual Report, 2002–03, p. 80–81); this percentage gradually increased to 100 in 1995-96 and then gradually increased further to 150 in 2002–03. Based on the above information we have adopted a straight line interpolation method to obtain estimates of marketing capital for the company, and, thereby, obtained refining capital stock from the estimate of total capital stock of the company.

Now coming to the estimates for IOC and HPCL for 2002–03, we probably have no better alternative to assuming that their marketing operations use capital in a way similar to BPCL. Given this assumption we use the same straight line interpolation method for these companies as in the case of BPCL. We have obtained the quantities marketed, when data are not available directly, by comparing the value of sales of the three companies and actual quantity sold by the BPCL that is available from its Annual Report for 2002–03. The refining capital stock has been taken as the residual after deduction of marketing capital from total capital stock.

Table 6.4: Segregation of Fixed Assets According to Purposes

Item No. of Table-6.3		*(percentage of gross block)* Refining	*Marketing* Own product	Other's product
Item 2	Buildings and Railway Sideways	5.1	5.1	7.8
Item 4	Tanks and Pipelines	5.4	5.4	8.2
Item 5	Dispensing Pumps	0.0	1.8	2.7
Item 6	LPG Cylinders, etc	9.4	9.4	14.2
	Total	19.9	21.7	32.9

Source: Calculations based on BPCL Annual Report: 2002-03, p.100.

One point is worthy of mention here. We have obtained the marketing capital percentage by applying ratio of volume of sales to the volume of production on the marketing capital percentage worked out for the year 2002–03 for BPCL. Some caution was warranted here. Volume of production and sales are subject to some fluctuation and so is, *a fortiori*, their ratio. To guard our estimate of capital stock from swings in the ratio we have fitted a linear trend to the ratios and applied the trend values for the estimation of capital stock. Our estimates of refinery service capital indices for the six PSCs are given in the appendix to the chapter (Table A 6.3).[8]

Refinery Sector Employment Index

In order to obtain employment indices we have divided total employment into two categories—Supervisory and Non-Supervisory—and then took weighted total using weights 1 and 0.5 respectively. We do not have data on average wages of the two categories of workers. However, annual reports of companies present information on number of employees by scales of pay. From a rough calculation of average wages (it varies across companies) the above choice of weights does not seem to be too wide off the mark. The next task is division of employment between refinery and marketing operations.

Marketing of petroleum products is done mainly by four PSC's—the three behemoths: IOCL, HPCL and BPCL, and a relatively small marketing company, IBP. Even after entry of Reliance Petroleum Limited in the petroleum business the position has not changed substantially. Roughly a quarter of RIL products go to PSC's. Reliance exports almost one third of its product and has a larger captive consumption. Thus its share in retail business is rather low compared to its share in total production (RIL Annual Report, 2004–05, p. 23). The four public sector oil marketing companies account for almost 86% of the aggregate sale of petroleum products in India in 2003–04 (Indian Oil, Annual Report, P. F–7). This share must have been higher before the entry of Reliance. In order to allocate employment in oil marketing sector to the companies (since the companies themselves do not give the division of their employment between the refining and marketing business) we have taken the share of the four marketing PSC's to be 91% in the 1990's.

In order to distribute the PSC market share among the four marketing companies we first note that IBP's major interest has been in MS and HSD. In terms of the share of marketing outlets the company held a more or less steady 8.5% share throughout the 1990's; the percentage has

[8] As mentioned in Chapter 3, KRL was taken over by BPCL and no separate data for KRL is available at the company level since 2005–06. But since KRL has a single refinery in Kerala, BPCL data at the state level presented in Volume–1 of Public Enterprises Survey provides the required information for KRL.

increased a little recently (op.cit.). But the company had very little stake in LPG. Keeping this consideration in mind, as a rough approximation, we have allowed a share of 5% of overall marketing business to IBP. The rest of the share is allocated to the three behemoths—IOCL, HPCL and BPCL. We have allocated marketing shares to the three companies in proportion to their purchase of finished products and raw materials (crude) after allowing for bulk sales to IBP. This criterion shows a change of relative shares of the three companies—IOCL, HPCL and BPCL—gradually from 60:22:18 to 55:23:22 over to the last fifteen years before IBP was taken over by the IOCL in 2006–07. Finally, in 2008–09 the relative shares became roughly 57:22:21.

After obtaining estimates of marketing employment of the three companies from the industry level marketing employment we can find refining employment by deducting marketing employment from total employment. The last point to be noted is that, for the above purpose we take rather arbitrarily only 95% of marketing employment for segregation from refining employment. This is necessary because product disposal would require some marketing employment in any case. Final estimates of refinery labour indices for the PSCs is given in the appendix to the chapter (Table A 6.2)

Measurement of Output

As already discussed in section–6.1, a refinery produces a good number of products that are classified into broad groups. The basic groups are Gasoline, Naphtha, LPG, Diesel, Kerosene and ATF. These are the products that every refinery wants to maximize. Apart from these items, some refineries produce lube base stock. Crude oil is valued basically because of the above products. By-products of the refining process are heavy ends. These are mostly low-value items. A part of refinery product is recycled as fuel and a small part is flared-up. Obviously, minimization of fuel-and-loss is a prime target of every refinery.

One can possibly think of four different measures of refinery production.

1. Throughput – i.e., the amount of crude processed.
2. Product – i.e., throughput less fuel-and-loss.
3. Distillate yield – i.e., product less heavy ends.

4. Refiner's margin which is akin to value added in refining operations. It is defined as the total value of products less the delivered cost of crude.

Throughput is the crudest measure; product is more refined. We have used product as our measure of refinery production. An alternative could be distillate yield; this is what refineries try to maximize. This measure ignores the by-products. Still it would be interesting. We, however, do not have data on this for all companies for at least a reasonable period time. As for gross refiner's margin, the problem is two-fold: i) available data do not allow us to distinguish between margins from refinery and marketing operations; ii) since the margin depends on price changes, comparability over time and across companies becomes problematic in the absence of sufficiently detailed data. So, we could not avail of this option. Output (product) indices for the six PSC's are given in the appendix (Table A 6.1).

Appendix

Table – A 6.1: Refinery Output of PSCs

	CPCL	*BPCL*	*HPCL*	*IOCL*	*KRL*	*NRL*
1991–92	5147	6630	8172	22970	4554	——
1992–93	4927	6875	9893	22967	4853	——
1993–94	5433	6831	9977	23255	4568	——
1994–95	6831	7071	9672	23545	4803	——
1995–96	5520	7065	10427	24025	7010	——
1996–97	6475	7279	10814	23606	6890	——
1997–98	6970	7591	8361	26037	7312	——
1998–99	6271	8531	8592	28664	7304	——
1999–00	6482	8433	9954	30385	7326	——
2000–01	6083	8203	11175	31033	7039	1451
2001–02	6225	8279	11563	31575	6398	2052
2002–03	6289	8221	12046	32810	7063	1665
2003–04	6472	8257	12852	35029	7419	1961
2004–05	8130	8598	13361	34042	7387	1834
2005–06	9413	9627	13332	35441	6456	1918
2006–07	9450	11234	15763	40089	7237	2227
2007–08	9318	11884	15804	43382	7687	2278
2008–09	9251	11437	15904	45415	7192	1992

Source: Indian Petroleum and Natural Gas Statistics, GoI, different issues.

Table – A 6.2: Refinery Labour Index for PSCs

	CPCL	*BPCL*	*HPCL*	*IOCL*	*KRL*	*NRL*
1991–92	1015	2739	3465	11147	809	—
1992–93	1033	2365	3290	10529	833	—
1993–94	1109	2340	3250	10556	864	—
1994–95	1193	2883	3741	12063	898	—
1995–96	1251	2593	3423	11371	976	—
1996–97	1216	2669	3357	11079	1022	—
1997–98	1178	2883	3529	11506	1064	—
1998–99	1176	2763	3093	10381	1320	—
1999–00	1174	2817	3068	10956	1294	—
2000–01	1145	2836	3108	11667	1290	447
2001–02	1142	2783	2578	11240	1294	464
2002–03	1132	3069	2585	11885	1173	467
2003–04	1163	2959	2427	11843	1264	487
2004–05	1185	2998	2169	11429	1255	491
2005–06	1172	2339	2053	9458	1238	510
2006–07	1187	2521	2387	10042	1230	527
2007–08	1201	2321	2182	10127	1245	589
2008–09	1222	2677	2834	13242	1260	582

Source: Public Enterprises Survey, Vol. II, different issues.

Table – A 6.3: Refinery Service Capital Index for PSCs

	CPCL	*BPCL*	*HPCL*	*IOCL*	*KRL*	*NRL*
1991–92	96116	163954	221404	467254	69302	—
1992–93	106064	172120	236851	507604	68058	—
1993–94	120027	182100	257420	555414	73293	—
1994–95	148251	195884	281073	579985	102228	—
1995–96	165389	209943	297038	680628	101749	—
1996–97	162603	220872	322788	785304	108148	—
1997–98	160932	257224	371263	904966	111636	—
1998–99	155815	280291	403086	1063973	113925	—
1999–00	188068	323059	531111	1309326	166135	—
2000–01	182894	341351	545650	1434924	167588	126056
2001–02	182300	353505	572772	1482458	173282	123774
2002–03	188271	355008	575904	1610186	173814	121462
2003–04	272798	367513	583411	1632556	173159	119228
2004–05	323115	384826	611983	1691049	179320	122524
2005–06	322378	432194	622301	1775500	197934	122061
2006–07	307917	439698	668751	2093097	214161	132435
2007–08	312686	445124	762969	2095116	224217	132476
2008–09	313238	463401	757966	2202037	256505	131560

Source: Computed as discussed in section 6.4.

Chapter 7

Technical Efficiency in Oil Refining Public Sector Companies

Over all this hangs the ubiquitous issue of quality change. The problem is general and pervasive.

Griliches, Z., 1992

Introduction

The petroleum scenario has gone through deep changes in India as swell as over the whole world over the last six decades. We have discussed the scenario in the Indian context in some detail in Chapter 3. After Independence the Import Parity Pricing (IPP) was naturally adopted as the country was basically dependent on imports and private operators. Gradually the degree of self-sufficiency improved but the oil price shock of 1973–74 came as a destabilizer. A desire for price stability and the political necessity to provide relief to the poor and common masses led the government to move to Administered Pricing Mechanism (APM) in 1976. Oil-Pool fund, set up as a part of the APM, was supposed to provide a cushion to the refining and marketing companies, but it proved to be an inadequate mechanism in the face of sustained and steep rise in price of crude; and oil-bonds issued by the government to meet the Oil-Pool deficits contributed significantly to government debt. That, along with the growing realisation that retention pricing under the APM sapped all competitive spirit, has led to decontrol of oil prices. While this is the context, our interest in the present paper is in the implication of the APM with respect to the operating efficiency of the refineries. To be more specific, we compare technical efficiency of refineries over two stretches of nine years before and after the dismantling of the APM.

The APM regime started to be undone in 1998 and was abandoned in 2002.[1] However, again in the face of sustained and steep rises in crude prices government intervention in fixing prices of petro-products came back in 2004 and continues even today only modified by the recent decision to partially decontrol. For our purpose it is important to

[1] A comprehensive discussion is given in Govt. of India, 2010.

distinguish between the APM and price control. Dismantling of the APM led to reverting back to the IPP. Price control reintroduced after 2004 did not do away with the idea of IPP that remained effective for the refineries. Only it led to subsidization of the oil marketing companies (OMCs) by the upstream companies (ONGC, GAIL, OIL) and the government. It is a different matter that subsidization was in fact incomplete. But the following two points are important for our present discussion.

1. The APM, prevalent earlier, compensated the public sector companies (PSCs) on the basis of a cost-plus formula. A compensation for costs and return on investments was guaranteed. This was the retention concept. In the whole scheme of things there was practically no incentive for cost minimization through competition among refineries. This really encouraged gold-plating of costs and creative accounting.
2. Under the APM the product-mix of refineries would be fixed by government directives. Thus the refineries had no incentive to achieve efficiency either by product or by input substitution. A general atmosphere of government directives and assured profits sapped the entrepreneurial spirit. In such a situation even the investments undertaken would not be based on rigorous long term real economic considerations but as a response to the prevailing situation with distorted incentives.[2]

These features of the APM did not come back after the dismantling of the APM at the end of the last decade even with reappearance of government control of prices. Price control at this later stage affected only the OMCs' marketing operations. Refineries were paid IPP prices. This meant that the refineries, now without assured profits, had every incentive to optimize resource use.[3] Further, the PSCs had now before them the

---

[2] I was told of some stories supporting the last point by Mr. S. Dasgupta, who served as General Manager (Finance) in NRL.

[3] To take one concrete example, Bongaigaon Refinery (BRPL) was making profits under the APM. However, this disappeared during 2000–01 and 2001–02 due to the operation of market-driven prices. So, BRPL, somehow handicapped by problems of supply of the basic raw-material, was under great pressure to make product and input substitution and optimization to make itself viable (Boro, 2004). Though BRPL is outside our purview here, the story is definitely not out of context.

example of a private sector refinery—the RPL Jamnagar refinery (started in 1999–2000). So, one would expect that the incentives and peer pressure should goad the refining companies to improve efficiency after the dismantling of the APM. Since the dismantling started in 1998 and it was supposed to take four years to complete the process, somewhat arbitrarily we take the mid-point, end of 1999-00, as the break point to study if efficiency changes did really take place after the date.

7.1 Earlier Studies on Performance of Oil Refining PSCs

In the above context here we take a brief overview of earlier studies on the performance of the oil refining PSCs. Bhattacharya and Datta (2005) undertook an experience curve analysis for the oil refining PSCs for the period 1978–79 to 1997–98. The study used an autoregressive distributed lag model to estimate the impact of experience and expansion of scale of operation on real unit cost at the company level, but without segregation of refining and distribution activities. We quote form the study: "It is normally presumed that in the course of exposure to repetitive tasks, the agents learn from experience to perform the tasks more quickly and efficiently. The learning effect need not be confined to the quality of workers and the operations management of the plant only. Experience may also affect machines in the sense that they may undergo series of technical improvements and in some cases may be replaced altogether by machines embodying upgraded technologies. … From the point of view of cost of production, the impact of experience is progressive when it leads to a gradual reduction in cost. The literature on the subject bears many examples of continuous cost reductions, in different degrees in different industries".

The study concludes: "Without any exception, we find that experience or exposure, wherever statistically significant as a regressor, exerts its influence by raising unit cost. This is contrary to common sense. Where experience is neutral, diminishing returns play an important role." In fact, the latter part of the observation is also contrary to the general perception among technicians that the technology of oil-refining does not support the hypothesis of diminishing returns. But here we are dealing with companies of which the bigger ones are multi-plant firms. So, diminishing returns is not beyond possibility. An important point is that the experience curve analysis is based on the hypothesis of competitive cost-minimizing firms and this hypothesis is alien to the reality of the PSCs during the 80s and 90s—the period to which the study under consideration was limited. On the basis of the above study one is tempted to conclude that the finding indicates growing inefficiency in all the public sector oil refining companies in India over roughly the last two decades of the previous century, which period belongs to the APM regime.

The above conclusion finds support in an earlier study of public profitability by Bhattacharya and Datta (2004). The occurrence of comfortable profits all through the period along with rising real unit cost of production is a phenomenon that needs to be carefully explained. The notion of public profit, an alternative criterion of performance evaluation based on shadow prices, i.e., prices based on opportunity cost to discount for build-up of prices due to non-market considerations, despite the possible crudity of available shadow prices, becomes relevant here. The basic idea is that the PSCs may have some commitments not guided by market considerations and so the pursuit of commercial profit, though important, may not be the overwhelming objective (Sen, 1983).

The idea behind public profitability is that it should measure the performance of an enterprise abstracting from the volatility of the market (or impositions by regulators) causing all sorts of price fluctuations and taking into account all sorts of operating costs, actually incurred or imputed, so that performance is not viewed as a function of public policy. The logic of shadow prices is that the criterion must discount, to the extent possible, for non-market considerations creeping into the decisions of a public sector company.[4] The above mentioned study concludes that public profitability, the concept used as an indicator of operational efficiency, declined for all the companies during the APM phase to which the study was confined. Of course, the decline was precipitate at certain stretches of time but moderate at others; and sharper for some companies compared to others as one would expect.

The above studies related to the last two decades of the APM but not the post-APM period, as we have mentioned. So, it remains interesting to

---

[4] The approach became popular in the late 70s and the 80s. For references see Bhattacharya and Datta, 2004.

check whether the IPP regime led to a change in the performance of the refining companies. But before going into that question we should note that in spite of careful analysis of available data both the above mentioned studies contained deficiencies in several respects. Firstly, the studies did not distinguish between the refining and marketing operations. So, the pure refiners (CPCL and KRL) were studied with the same yardstick as refiners-cum-marketers (IOCL, HPCL and BPCL). Secondly, measurements of all the variables—output, labour and capital—involve intricate considerations, as we have discussed in the previous chapter. The studies left scope for much improvement in these respects.

This challenge was taken up to a great extent in Datta (2008) where data up to 2004-05 were considered. If we consider the end of 1999-2000 as the break-point for the APM, then data for only five post-APM years were available for the study.[5] But even with such data limitations it found some, though rather weak, evidence of improvement in technical efficiency in the PSCs during the short post-APM phase. The evidence was crucially dependent on the inclusion of NRL in the study though this result is not straight forward to explain logically; NRL—the smallest PSC—was found to be also the least efficient unit, and it started operating only in the post-APM phase. It is in this background that we have taken up the present study. Now we have data for four additional post-APM years up to 2008-09 and this should help us get a more definite answer to the basic question posed here: is there a significant difference in the performance of the oil refining PSCs between the APM and post-APM regimes? The answer we have got now on the basis of the larger data-set is an emphatic "yes" and that is what we discuss in the following sections.

Here we should repeat a caveat sounded in Chapter 4. In Stochastic Frontier Analysis (SFA) inefficiency is measured by the distance between the actual performance and an estimated frontier of achievable output. The frontier is basically determined by the best performing among units of different size classes. The idea is that lag in performance reflects inefficiency in resource use while, in fact, the lag also depends

---

[5] The study includes six PSC's: Indian Oil Corporation (IOCL), Hindusthan Petroleum Corporation Limited (HPCL), Bharat Petroleum Corporation Limited (BPCL), Chennai Petroleum Corporation Limited (CPCL), Numaligarh Refineries Limited (NRL) and Kochi Refineries Limited (KRL).

on other influences like technical progress and economy of scale. SFA allows inclusion of a time variable in the production function purporting to account for technical change. However, this option is generally avoided, as we also do here, for doubts regarding the ability of the regression, in the case to time varying technical efficiency, to churn out and segregate the right information from two time variables used in the same expression. This means that our result really has to be interpreted as a mixture of technical efficiency and other influences mentioned above though the literature is not always very careful to point this out. Following the literature we also indulge in this inaccuracy of expression consciously and use the term technical efficiency for what the results stand for.

7.2 Production and Inputs

The Production Function

Before taking up the estimation of technical efficiencies we need to discuss conceptual questions of representation of the production function in the specific context of oil refineries. One way of viewing the aim of productivity studies (the approach we have taken here) is judging how efficiently inputs are being exploited to obtain output. So, the basic variables that have to be tackled are output (Y) and inputs. Inputs include material (or, intermediate) inputs (M) apart from the primary inputs—capital (K) and labour (L). For refineries the predominant material input is crude. It accounts for roughly 90% of cost of production and 95% of total intermediate input cost.[6] So, for practical purposes, it may not be a big mistake if we take it to represent the sole intermediate input.

We take the stochastic frontier approach which stands on the underlying notion of a production function, which we may write as:

$$Y = F(M, K, L) \qquad ...(7.1)$$

It is generally supposed that the material input enters the production function in a way different from that of primary inputs. In this sense oil

[6] It can be verified from the profit and loss accounts given in Volume-III of Public Enterprises Survey.

refineries seem to present a suitable case for a separable production function.[7] Product of refineries by weight maintains a rather stable relationship with the amount of crude processed (throughput) despite big changes in capital intensities over time;[8] so much so, that throughput is often used as an index of output of refineries[9] (though we will take a slightly refined concept of product). This means that M does not enter into any substitutability relationship with other inputs. To emphasize this point we may represent the production function to be separable in material and primary inputs; so, it takes the form:

$$Y = F_1(K, L) + F_2(M) \qquad \text{...(7.2)}$$

Clearly, the equation implies that the two terms on the RHS are expressed in the same unit as Y. Thus K and L have their units, but through F_1-transformation they are converted to value-added in terms of output. The same is true of F_2. In the case of oil refineries the physical units of Y and M are the same as they are expressed in weights, but they are qualitatively different. Naturally, we cannot equate the same quantities of the two – just as we cannot add apples and oranges. We may refer to the units in the two cases as product-unit and crude-unit respectively. F_2 transformation is supposed to convert crude-units to product-units. Remembering the constant ratio $(1/\theta)$ between Y and M we will represent the conversion from crude-unit to product-unit by a scalar factor .[10] So, we write:

---

[7] The concept of value added becomes easier to handle when separability exists between raw material and primary inputs (Arrow, 1974). Also, in this case the production function may be assumed to take a simpler form.

[8] Throughput to output ratio sometimes varies significantly across refineries. The most plausible explanation seems to be varying sources and, therefore, quality of crude.

[9] This means that there is no significant substitutability between capital and labour on the one hand and material input on the other. This property may not be so clearly present in some other production processes. Arrow (1974) mentions power generation where higher use of capital may economize on the use of fuel, thus suggesting substitutability between capital and material input.

[10] This really means conversion to equivalent value which we measure in output units instead of money.

$$Y = F_1(K, L) + \quad M, \text{ or, } Y = F_1(K, L) + \quad Y \qquad ...(7.3)$$

This simplifies to $Y = f(K, L)$. ...(7.4)

Normally, in this form of production functions the dependent variable should be the value added. But, unlike F_1, f is not a value added function; f-transformation gives physical output. So, we are able to take Y as the directly observed real product and avoid intricate questions of computation of real value added. It is a great advantage.

We may, however, note here that physical measures of output do not take into account quality changes. To introduce that we might write $Ye^{\mu t}$ in place of Y, where μ stands for the steady rate of quality change; but we will avoid that to overcome difficulties in quality measurement.[11] Obviously, this will mean an underestimation of production and any evidence of improvement in technical efficiency over time in spite of this underestimation will mean that the evidence is, in fact, stronger than observed. Let us now turn briefly to the problem of measurement of variables discussed in detail in the previous chapter.

Measurement of Output

A refinery produces a good number of products that are classified into broad groups. The major groups are Gasoline, Naphtha, LPG, Diesel, Kerosene and ATF.[12] These are the products that every refinery wants to maximize. Apart from these items, some refineries produce lube base stock. Crude oil is valuable basically because of its above products. By-products of the refining process are heavy ends - mostly low-value items. A tiny fraction of refinery product is recycled as fuel or flared-up. Obviously, minimization of fuel-and-loss is a prime target of every refinery. Under the circumstances one can consider at least four different measures of refinery production as discussed earlier.

For considerations already discussed we have used product as our measure of refinery output.

---

[11] A discussion of the problems of measurement may be found in Heravi and Silver, 2007.

[12] LPG is liquefied petroleum gas and ATF is aviation turbine fuel.

Primary Inputs

Data on the primary inputs—capital and labour—are not available at the plant level; whatever data are available relate basically to the company level. This makes us constrained to work with company level data. Fortunately, there is some information that can form some basis for separation of factor employment in refining and marketing segments. We have explained in the next section how we have approached the task. In what follows we explain our measurement of variables at the company level.

Estimation of Service Capital Index

The available estimates of fixed assets (or gross block) given by annual reports of companies are calculated at historical prices, i.e., neither at current nor at constant prices. However, changes in gross block are at current prices. These changes give direct and more reliable information on capital formation than figures on investment in fixed capital, because investments take some time to be transformed into capital stock. Using changes in gross block[13] we have estimated indices of service capital index following the method suggested by Datta (2006). The idea here is to measure capital stock in efficiency units, which is supposed to be proportional to the service received from the stock. Estimation of service capital indices has been discussed in detail in the previous chapter.[14]

[13] Data are available from Public Enterprises Survey, GOI. It may be noted that data on Kochi refineries after its merger with the BPCL in April, 2004, is available from state-wise distribution of PSCs.

[14] As the first step we use the implicit price deflator of Net Fixed Capital Stock for the Public Sector Registered Manufacturing obtained from CSO estimates to deflate changes in gross block. The next step is to decide on the average lifetime of assets. The international standard is to take average lifetime of refinery capital stock to be 20 years (Gary and Handwerk, 2001, p. 361). But we have taken it to be 22 years on the consideration that scarcity of capital and relatively cheap labour in India would lead to more intensive maintenance and longer life of equipments in the country. Further, we have taken the terminal efficiency to be 2/3rd of that of the new stock. This is indeed arbitrary. But the implicit terminal efficiency under PIM with life time of 20 years and a rate of time preference = 10% is 1/3 (Datta, 2006). Oil refining technology being a very sophisticated one a much higher terminal efficiency seems to be appropriate.

Estimation of Labour Index

In order to obtain employment indices we have divided total employment into two categories—Supervisory and Non-Supervisory—and then took weighted total using weights 1.0 and 0.5 respectively. We do not have data on average wages of the two categories of workers. However, annual reports of companies present information on number of employees by scales of pay. From a rough calculation of average wages (it varies across companies) the above choice of weights does not seem to be too wide off the mark. Details of the estimation procedure are given in the previous chapter.

7.3 Factor Employment in Refining Operations and Partial Productivities

Segregation of Refining and Marketing Operations

After arriving at total factor employment by companies our problem is to segregate them between the refining and marketing segments for companies undertaking both the operations This is necessary to make data comparable across companies, some of which are, so to say, pure refiners and others undertaking both refining of crude and marketing of their own as well as others' products. As data for the two categories of activities are not available readily, we depend on the clue provided by the BPCL Annual Report (2002–03). For other companies even this clue is not available. We have applied the BPCL clue for the IOCL and the HPCL as well and we have assumed that capital stock required for marketing operations by the three companies is proportional to the volume of operation.[15]

It transpires from an analysis of the report that roughly 55% of the capital stock of BPCL in 2002–03 belonged to its marketing operation. We further note that BPCL sales was almost 60% higher than its own production in 1990–91 (Annual Report, 2002–03, p. 80–81); this percentage gradually increased to 100 in 1995–96 and then gradually increased further to 150 in 2002–03. Based on the above information we have adopted a straight line interpolation method to obtain estimates of marketing capital for the company and, thereby, obtained refining capital stock from the estimate of total capital stock of the company. Now coming to the estimates for IOCL and HPCL for 2002–03, we have

[15] An implication is that inefficiency in marketing operations will impact our analysis of the relevant company's refining operations.

obtained the quantities marketed, when data are not available directly, by comparing the value of sales of the three companies and actual quantities sold by the BPCL that is available from its Annual Report for 2002-03. We use the same straight line interpolation method for these companies as in the case of BPCL. The refining capital stock has then been taken as the residual after deduction of marketing capital from total capital stock[16] for all the years covered by the study.

As regards labour, companies provide information regarding total company-wide employment only and the Ministry concerned provides information regarding industry-wide employment separately for refining and distribution operations. We have distributed total employment in the marketing sector of the industry among the PSCs in proportion to the volume of their marketing operations. After obtaining estimates of marketing employment of the three refining cum marketing companies from the industry level marketing employment, as discussed in the previous chapter, we obtained refining employment by deducting each company's marketing employment from its total employment.

Partial Factor Productivities

Figures 7.1 and 7.2 show capital and labour productivities respectively in the refining segments of the PSCs concerned. In the Appendix Tables A 7.1 and A 7.2 present estimates of partial productivities[17] and

---

[16] We have obtained the marketing capital percentage by applying ratio of volume of sales to the volume of production on the marketing capital percentage worked out for the year 2002-03 for BPCL. Some caution was warranted here. Volume of production and sales are subject to some fluctuation and so is, a fortiori, their ratio. To guard our estimate of capital stock from swings in the ratio we have fitted a linear trend to the ratio and applied the trend values for the estimation of capital stock.

[17] Productivity is defined as the ratio between output and input. Normally several factors are used in production. So, a "total input" index (involving aggregation problem) is required to obtain a measure of total factor productivity (TFP). When only labour or capital is used as the measure of input we obtain (average) labour or capital productivities. To underline the partial nature of these input measures we refer to them as partial productivities. Because of their intuitive appeal partial productivities are very commonly used in the literature (Krishna, 1987; Foley and Michl, 1999). Productivity measures are often expressed as indices to give a clear view of changes over time.

Table A 7.3 gives capital intensity in the refining segment of the six public sector companies. A close look at Figure 7.1 (and also Table A 7.1) suggests that roughly a couple of years into the second half of the period under consideration (the post-APM phase) the curves, in general, have rather stopped declining and flattened out. And, roughly speaking, somewhat the opposite observation seems to be valid for labour productivity as seen from Figure 7.2 (and Table A 7.2). After maintaining a roughly flat trend in most of the cases the curves seem to have taken an upward turn, mildly in most cases but quite sharply in some cases, though labour productivity declined for all companies during the last year under study. This generates special interest in the comparison of technical efficiency trend over the two phases. Flattening out of capital productivity and rising labour productivity indicates a break from the past trend when capital productivity was generally declining and labour productivity was relatively flat. Of course, changes in factor productivities were not steady. Table A 7.3 shows that all the five major companies show quite significant increase in capital intensity (K/L) over the whole period, as one would expect from the observations on capital and labour productivities. We will now check what story SFA makes out of the above facts.

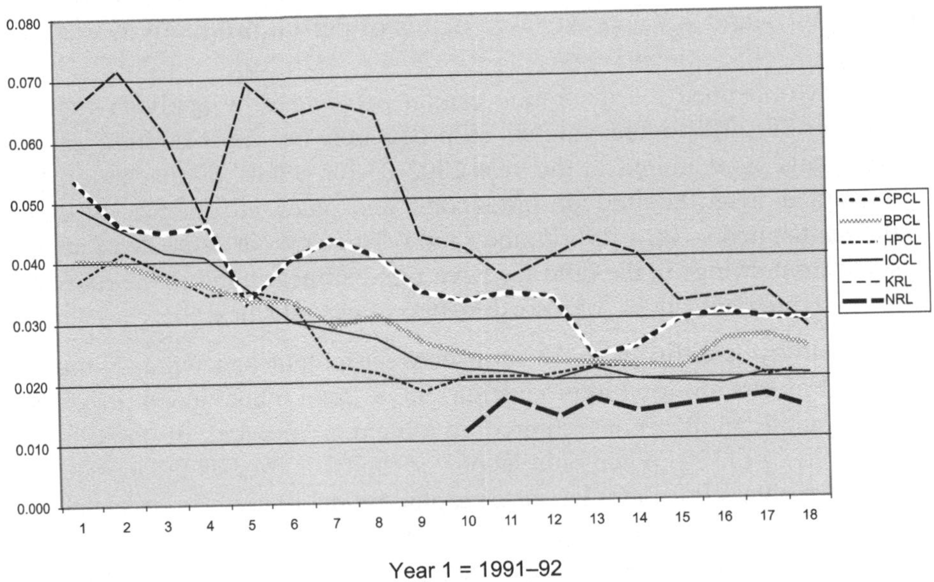

Fig. 7.1: Capital Productivity

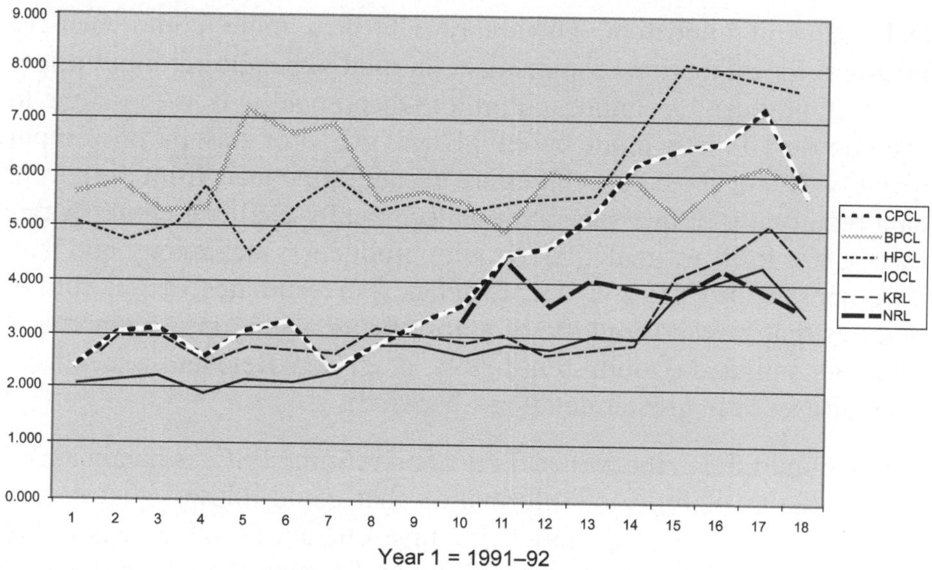

Fig. 7.2: Labour Productivity

7.4 Technical Efficiency in Oil Refining PSCs

Technical Efficiency and Allocative Efficiency

Study of efficiency in a multifaceted real work environment is a very complex task. To make the task manageable and meaningful economists approach the problem from an abstract setting. The basic idea is that fully efficient technical operation gives the highest feasible level of product from a given set of resources. This gives the idea of a production frontier. Following our discussion in section-III we will characterize it as: $Y = f(K, L),\ f_K, f_L > 0, f_{KK}, f_{LL} < 0.$ A producer is said to be technically inefficient unless he operates on the frontier. Distance of actual achievement from the frontier forms the basis for the measurement of technical efficiency.

This notion is silent about the choice of factor combination. If there is substitutability among productive factors the combination in which they are used in production should depend on relative prices. So, there is a question of efficient choice of factor combinations. Here comes the notion of input allocative efficiency. Unless a producer is fully efficient following both the above notions he has scope to improve. The cost frontier, which is the dual of the production frontier, is capable of taking into account loss of efficiency due to both the possible failures—

technical and allocative. Obviously, CE is a more comprehensive measure. Its estimation requires data on total expenditure, input prices and output quantity indices. Further, theoretically it is possible to decompose CE into input based TE and AE. For this purpose input quantity data or input cost shares are needed. But, apart from the severe data requirements, this separation is technically challenging as, in this case, CE is to be estimated along with production technology and then decomposed into TE and AE. Efficiency of estimates of CE further requires that prices should vary across firms, which is a requirement often not satisfied (Coelli *et al.*, 1998, p. 211).[18] Relevant issues have been discussed in greater detail in Chapter 5.

Estimation of CE in the present case of oil refining PSCs is handicapped by the non-availability of information that could allow separation of expenditures in refining and marketing operations on a reasonably reliable basis. Secondly, price of crude fluctuates a lot and varies according to source. Different plants use crude from one or more sources making estimation of an average annual price of crude, required for estimation of CE, difficult. Therefore, we confine ourselves to the estimation of output based technical efficiency (Kumbhakar and Lovell, 2000).

The Model to be Estimated

The most commonly used forms of production function are trans-log and Cobb-Douglas models which are given as:

Trans-log: $\ln Y_i = \beta_0 + \beta_1 \ln K_i + \beta_2 \ln L_i + \beta_3(\ln K_i)^2 + \beta_4(\ln Li)^2 + \beta_5 \ln K_i.\ln L_i +$ ...(7.5)

Cobb-Douglas: $\ln Y_i = \beta_0 + \beta_1 \ln K_i + \beta_2 \ln L_i + (v_i - u_i)$ ...(7.6)

Abbreviating the production function we can write our model to be estimated as:

$$Y_i = F(X_i, \beta)\ \exp(v_i) TE_i \qquad ...(7.7)$$

18 The relevance of the concept of allocative efficiency, though theoretically very nice and interesting, in the context of petroleum refineries is not very clear. No two refineries are identical. Though all the refineries refine crude oil (not of identical quality), the products are not identical. Plant design and factor requirements vary according to differences in thrusts in output and once a plant is set up there is very little scope of factor substitution.

where y is the output, x and β stand for the vector of arguments of the production function and the vector of the coefficients respectively; all the variables being expressed in logarithm. v is the random error term and subscript i refers to the particular cross section. Further, firm specific technical efficiency which is assumed to be a random variable, may be written as: . $TE_i = \exp(-u_i)$. $TE_i \leq 1$, so, $u_i \geq 0$, i.e., this error is one-sided. So, we can write (7.7) as:

$$Y_i = F(X_i, \beta) \exp(v_i) \exp(-u_i) \qquad \text{...(7.8)}$$

Here the assumptions are that $v_i \sim IID\ N(0, \sigma_v^2)$ and $u_i \sim IID$ $N^+(\mu, \sigma_u^2)$. Further, u_i and v_i are independent of each other and also independent of x_i. So, the underlying model is Normal-Truncated Normal; it was introduced by Stevenson (1980).

Our objectives are to (i) estimate the vector β of $F(X_i, \beta)$ under a specific assumption on the form of the production function, and (ii) estimate the technical efficiency of each producer (e^{-u_i}, or simply u_i). In the case of panel data technical efficiency may be assumed either to be time invariant or as varying with time. If the panel is a long one the assumption of time invariance may not be defensible unless specifically suggested by data. Battese and Coelli (1992) proposed a model for time varying technical inefficiency for stochastic frontier approach with panel data. Technical inefficiency effects for N cross-sections observed over T periods are defined by:

$$u_{it} = [e^{-\eta(t-T)}]u_i, \qquad i = 1,2,\ldots N;\ t = 1,2,\ldots T; \qquad (7.9)$$

Where u_i's are assumed to be IID truncated normal random variables as defined above and η, which is the focus of our attention, is an unknown scalar to be estimated. Maximum-likelihood estimation of equation (7.9) has been implemented in the FRONTIER programme that we use in the present study.[19] The programme estimates the vector β, η as well as $\gamma(= \sigma_u / \sigma$, where $\sigma^2 = \sigma_u^2 + \sigma_v^2), \gamma$ lies between 0 and 1 depending on the dominance of σ_v or σ_u respectively.

---

[19]For guidance to the programme see Coelli, 1996.

Trend in Technical Efficiency

Implementation of the above model requires assumption of the form of the production function. In order to verify whether results are susceptible to the assumption of a particular form we have implemented both the flexible trans-log form and the relatively simple Cobb-Douglas form using panel data. The cross-sections consisted of the five major oil refining companies and the smaller company, NRL, also in the public sector. The first panel consisted of all the six cross-sections, five of them repeated for eighteen years from 1991–92 to 2008–09. Production in NRL started only in 2000–01, so we have nine missing observations (from 1991–92 to 1999–2000) in this panel. The second panel had all the six companies repeated nine times from 2000–01 to 2008–09, which corresponds to the post-APM regime. Thus two models of production function for each of two panels result in four regressions numbered 1 to 4. The results are presented in Table 7.1.

We also ran a second set of regressions on the models with truncations of the two panels. The objective here is to exclude some possibilities. The truncation of the first panel takes nine years from 1991–92 to 1999–2000 for all the five major companies (it is the period corresponding to the APM regime; NRL was not in the picture then). It gives us regressions 5 and 6 corresponding to the two models. Next we consider a truncation of the second panel, excluding NRL, i.e., we consider all the five major companies over the post-APM nine years in regressions-7 and 8. Our intention behind the two regressions, 7 and 8, is to check whether the inclusion of NRL in the later half had any decisive role in the difference in the trends of efficiency, as observed, over the two time periods. The results are presented in Table 7.2.

We have already noted that the technical efficiency has been taken to vary with time as in equation (7.9). Regression–1 gives the Maximum-Likelihood estimates for the trans-log model using the first panel. Regression–2 gives the same for the Cobb-Douglas Model. Results of the two regressions can be seen from Table 7.1. The first point to note here is that estimates of $\tilde{a}$ for both the models are very close to unity. This means that the one-sided error term (due to inefficiency) dominates the composite error. LR test of one-sided error is also highly significant. We may note that this statistic has a mixed chi-square distribution. The critical value obtained from Table–1 of Kodde and Palm (1986) is 7.045 at 5% level of significance for degrees of freedom equal to 3; this strongly rejects the null hypothesis of no technical inefficiency for both the regressions. As for the trend in technical efficiency, we note that estimated is positive and statistically significant at one percent level for trans-log and five percent level for Cobb-Douglas models, i.e., the null hypothesis that η is zero is rejected for both the models. So, we can legitimately observe that there is important preliminary evidence of a falling trend in inefficiency over the whole period under consideration. This finding is not particular to the form of the production function.

Table 7.1: ML Estimates of Production Function and Technical Efficiency Coefficients

	First Panel (No. of Observations = 99		*Second Panel (No. of Observations = 54)*	
Coefficients	*Tr.log Regression-1*	*C.D. Regression-2*	*Tr.log Regression-3*	*C.D. Regression-4*
	6.935	0.922	7.114	0.017
	(6.186)**	(6.654)**	(7.422)**	(0.108)
	–4.783	0.398	–3.393	0.693
	(–7.238)**	(13.22)**	(-6.042)**	(16.23)**
	5.145	0.285	2.622	0.0.059
	(4.881)**	(7.245)**	(3.023)*	(0.861)
	0.836		3.991	
	(8.156)**		(1.682)	
	0.277		–0.273	
	(2.220)*		(–0.477)	
	–1.206		–0.121	
	(–7.395)**		(-0.171)	
	0.072	0.113	0.009	0.094
	(0.854)	(1.579)	(0.485)	(1.337)
	0.979	0.981	0.891	0.987
	(34.71)**	(74.59)**	(4.533)**	(12.96)**
	–0.531	–0.665	.035	–0.609
	(–0.695)	(–2.098)*	(6.01)**	(–1.675)
	0.0304	0.0200	0.035	0.0366
	(3.449)**	(2.145)*	(1.320)	(3.427)**
Log likelihood function	168.30	149.02	90.90	92.18
LR test of one sided error (No. of restrictions = 3)	147.44**	144.11**	63.58**	102.70**

Figures in parentheses relate to the t-statistic. *means significant at 5% level and ** means significant at 1% level for one-tailed test.

A study of relative superiority of the trans-log over the Cobb-Douglas model can be made using the log-likelihood functions. The value of the generalized likelihood-ratio statistic for testing the null hypothesis that the coefficients of the second order terms of the trans-log model are jointly insignificant (i.e., $\beta_{ij} = 0$) is:

$$\text{L.R.} = -2\{\text{Ln}(\text{L}_{\text{C–D}}) - \text{Ln}(\text{L}_{\text{T–L}})\}.$$

L.R. is here with 3 degrees of freedom (Coelli *et al.* P.218). The test results are presented in Table 7.3. The test yields insignificant result; so, we cannot prefer trans-log to the simpler form, though the point is only of academic interest in the present case as both the forms give us the same conclusion. However, as we will see below, the test consistently fails to attest the superiority of the trans-log model over the Cobb-Douglas model for all the panels in the present study.

Considering the results with the second panel that stretches over the post-APM period, 2000–01 to 2008–09, with six cross-sections, using the two models (regression–3 and regression–4, Table 7.1) it is notable that gamma coefficients for both the regressions are again very close to unity and LR tests of one-sided error are highly significant. 's for both the models are now higher but for the trans-log model it is statistically insignificant even at 5% level while, for the Cobb-Douglas model, it is statistically significant at 1% level. The value of the generalized likelihood-ratio statistic (Table 7.3) fails to reject the hypothesis that the second order terms of the trans-log model are ineffective. So, we can legitimately focus on the Cobb-Douglas model which suggests significant increasing trend (faster than that in the case of the first panel) in efficiency.

The finding of rising efficiency in the second panel suggests it should be interesting to check whether rising efficiency characterizes the whole eighteen-year period under study without any qualification, i.e., without much difference between the trends in the APM and the later period. For this purpose we run regressions with a truncation (the first nine-years) of the first panel. The Maximum-Likelihood estimates for the two models with this truncation of the first panel covering the APM phase are given in Table 7.2 (regression–5 and regressin–6).

Table 7.2: ML Estimates of Production Function and Technical Efficiency Coefficients

	Truncation of Panel-1 (No. of Observations = 45)		*Truncation of Panel-2 (No. of Observations = 45)*	
Coefficients	*Tr.log. Regression-5*	*C.D. Regression-6*	*Tr.log Regression-7*	*C.D. Regression-8*
	3.016 (3.036)** 2.850 (4.971)** –4.721 (-5.587)** –0.449 (–2.825)** 0.203 (0.939)* 0.671 (1.780)	1.219 (4.523)** 0.290 (3.389)** 0.372 (5.093)**	M.L. regression fails to yield any meaningful result.	0.204 (1.301) 0.598 (10.350)** 0.160 (2.256)**
	0.002 (4.315)** 0.009 (0.132) 0.009 (1.611) 0.129 (1.206)	0.014 (0.587) 0.896 (4.925)** 0.0067 (0.025) -0.019 (-0.596)		0.002 (0.846) 0.623 (1.419) 0.008 (8.849)** 0.116 (3.438)**
Log likelihood function	73.95	74.65		86.32
LR test of one sided error (No. of restrictions = 3)	1.05	44.05		39.47

Figures in parentheses relate to the t-statistic. * means significant at 5% level and ** means significant at 1% level for one-tailed test.

Interestingly, we observe that for both the models this phase **yields** ’s ***to be statistically insignificant.*** In fact, the trans-log model fails to yield a significant value for test statistic for one-sided error[20] and the value of

[20] The relevant value given by Kodde and Palm (1986) is 7.045. So, the regression does not seem to be good for verification of technical inefficiency.

is close to zero. The generalized log likelihood ratio test cannot reject the joint insignificance of the coefficients of second order terms of the trans-log model, which means that the second order terms of the trans-log model are not effective. Therefore, we can again, focus on the Cobb-Douglas model. This model suggests existence of one-sided error (inefficiency) and gives a negative value[21] for (declining efficiency?) though statistically insignificant. This is in sharp contrast to the results for the last nine years (post-APM regime) which show efficiency improving significantly (regressions 3 and 4 corresponding to the second panel). This suggests that the observed improving efficiency read from results of regressions 1 and 2 (for the whole period of eighteen years) really reflects the improving efficiency of the last nine years.

Table 7.3: Generalized Log-Likelihood Ratio Test of Significance of the Trans-Log Model

Panel	*Log-Likelihood Function*		*Natural Logarithm of L.L.Function*		*-2[ln(CD-ln(Tr.Log)]*
	CD	*Tr.log*	*Ln(CD)*	*Ln(Tr.log)*	*GLR*
First Panel: 6 cross-sections x 18 years: Reg.1 vs. Reg.2	149.03	168.3	5.0041	5.1257	0.24327
Second Panel: 6 cross-sections x last nine years: Reg. 3 vs. Reg. 4	92.18	90.90	4.5237	4.5098	–0.0279
Truncated first panel: 5 cross-sections x first nine years: Reg. 5 vs. Reg. 6	74.65	73.95	4.3128	4.3034	–0.0188
Truncated second panel: Regressions 7 and 8.	Regression–7 is ineffective; so no question of comparison with regression–8.				

To eliminate any doubt that the comparability between the first and the last nine years might have been affected by the inclusion of NRL in the later period we now turn our attention to a truncation of the second panel, i.e., the period 2000–01 to 2008–09, with the five major PSCs

21 This is consistent with findings of earlier studies discussed above, though the nine-year period covers only a part of the period covered by those studies.

excluding the NRL. Maximum-Likelihood regression for the trans-log model (regression–7) fails to yield any meaningful result (Table 7.2). However, Cobb-Douglas model verifies the existence of inefficiency and a positive and highly statistically significant . This is perfectly in conformity with the result of regression-4 (i.e., for panel–2). This suggests the finding of rising efficiency stands irrespective of whether we include or exclude NRL.

7.5 Conclusion

The study compares the performance of the oil refining PSCs of India between two stretches spanning over nine years; one ending with 1999–00 and the other beginning there. The earlier stretch is identified with the APM regime and the later stretch marks the post-APM regime. A visual observation of the trend of capital and labour productivities indicate an improvement in the performance of the PSCs in the later phase over that in the earlier phase. For a more rigorous study the SFA approach has been chosen.

Two forms of production function have been tried for the maximum likelihood estimation. The trans-log form, being a flexible one, is often preferred over the simpler Cobb-Douglas form but in all the four separate applications in the present study generalized likelihood ratio test fails to establish effectiveness of the second order terms of the trans-log form; in one case it does not give any meaningful result at all. Cobb-Douglas form gives good fit in all the cases. We have, however, presented results for both the forms anticipating academic interest of readers.

The basic findings may be summarized as follows:

1. Over the whole period of eighteen-years, results suggest a trend of improving performance in terms of what is referred to in the literature as technical efficiency.
2. When we confine our study to the first stretch corresponding to the APM regime, the evidence of rising efficiency absolutely vanishes. But for the later stretch corresponding to the post-APM regime the evidence of rising efficiency is strongly present. This suggests that the improving performance observed for the two stretches taken as a whole was the result of performance in the later stretch.

3. The finding of rising efficiency during the post-APM period remains valid even when we exclude the NRL, which company was not there in the panel for the earlier period. Thus the presence or absence of NRL in different panels is not instrumental for the finding of rising efficiency in the later period. In fact NRL, being an underperformer, it is not expected to influence the frontier very significantly and hence the performance of other companies in the SFA.
4. Economic reform undertaken in 1991 was not of any great significance to the public sector oil refineries but dismantling of the APM had an objective of enhancing efficiency of refinery operations. Our study shows strong evidence of the aim having been realized. Our results, moreover, seem to be more significant than they appear. Emphasis on product quality as well as maintenance of environmental norms has gradually gathered momentum and they have been strong particularly during the more recent period. While this generally meant use of more factor inputs per barrel of crude our measure of product does not account for quality improvement of products. This means efficiency improvements captured by our models are underestimates.
5. The above consideration strengthens the conclusion of the study that the policy of reform of pricing mechanism (retention pricing under the APM) of refined petroleum undertaken by the government of India towards the end of the 90s has really been successful in improving the efficiency of the public sector oil-refining companies in general. The finding strengthens the conclusion drawn by Datta (2008) on the basis of a smaller data base.

Appendix

Tables for Factor Productivities and Capital Intensity

Table A 7.1: Capital Productivity in Public Sector Refineries

	CPCL	*BPCL*	*HPCL*	*IOCL*	*KRL*	*NRL*
1991–92	0.054	0.040	0.037	0.049	0.066	
1993–94	0.045	0.038	0.039	0.042	0.062	
1995–96	0.033	0.034	0.035	0.035	0.069	
1997–98	0.043	0.030	0.023	0.029	0.065	
1999–00	0.034	0.026	0.019	0.023	0.044	
2000–01	0.033	0.024	0.020	0.022	0.042	0.012
2003–04	0.024	0.022	0.022	0.021	0.043	0.016
2005–06	0.029	0.022	0.021	0.020	0.033	0.016
2008–09	0.030	0.025	0.021	0.021	0.028	0.015

Source: Our calculations explained in the text.

Table A 7.2: Labour Productivity in Public Sector Refineries

	CPCL	*BPCL*	*HPCL*	*IOCL*	*KRL*	*NRL*
1991–92	5.07	2.42	2.36	2.06	5.63	
1993–94	4.90	2.92	3.07	2.20	5.29	
1995–96	4.41	2.72	3.05	2.11	7.19	
1997–98	5.92	2.63	2.37	2.26	6.88	
1999–00	5.52	2.99	3.24	2.77	5.66	
2000–01	5.31	2.89	3.60	2.66	5.46	3.25
2002–03	5.56	2.68	4.66	2.76	6.02	3.57
2004–05	6.86	2.87	6.16	2.98	5.89	3.74
2006–07	7.96	4.46	6.60	3.99	5.88	4.23
2008–09	7.57	4.27	5.61	3.43	5.71	3.43

Source: Our calculations explained in the text.

Table A 7.3: Capital Intensity in Public Sector Refineries

	CPCL	*BPCL*	*HPCL*	*IOCL*	*KRL*	*NRL*
1991–92	94.7	59.9	63.9	41.9	85.7	
1993–94	108.2	77.8	79.2	52.6	84.9	
1995–96	132.3	81.0	86.8	59.9	104.3	
1997–98	136.7	89.2	105.2	78.7	105.0	
1999–00	160.2	114.7	173.1	119.5	128.4	
2000–01	159.7	120.4	175.5	123.0	129.9	282.0
2002–03	166.3	115.7	222.8	135.5	148.2	260.4
2004–05	272.8	128.4	282.2	148.0	142.9	249.8
2006–07	259.4	174.4	280.2	208.4	174.1	251.5
2008–09	256.3	173.1	267.5	166.3	203.7	226.2

Source: Our calculations explained in the text.

REFERENCES

Aigner, D.J., Lovell, C.A.K. and Schnmidt, P. (1977), Formulation and Estimation of Stochastic Frontier Production Function Models, *Journal of Econometrics*, 6(1), July, 21-37.

Annual Report (2002-03), Bharat Petroleum Corporation Limited, India.

Annual Report (2004-05), Reliance Industries Limited, India.

Arrow, K.J. (1974), The Measurement of Real Value Added, in *Nations and Households in Economic Growth,* eds., David, P.A and Reder, M.W., Academic Press, N. York.

Bandyopadhyay, D and A. Das (2008), Identifiability of Stochastic Frontier Models, *Journal of Quantitative Economics*, 6 (1&2), January-July.

Battese, G.E., and T. J. Coelli (1988), Prediction of Firm Level Technical Efficiencies with a Generalized Frontier Production Function and Panel Data, *Journal of Econometrics*, 38, 387-399.

Battese, G.E., and T. J. Coelli (1992), Frontier Production Functions, Technical Efficiency and Panel Data: With Application to Paddy Farmers in India, *Journal of Productivity Analysis*, 3, 153-169.

Bhattacharya, P. and Datta, M. (2004), Public Profitability in Oil-Refining PSC's, *Economic and Political Weekly*, May 29, Mumbai.

Bhattacharya, P. and Datta, M. (2005), The Story of Experience in Petro-Refining in India, in Ghosh, R and Neogi, C. (eds), *Theory and Application of Productivity and Efficiency: Econometric and DEA Approach*, Macmillan India Limited, N. Delhi.

Blades, D. (2001), *Measuring Capital: A manual on the Measurement of Capital Stocks, Consumption of fixed Capital and Capital Services*, OECD, Paris.

Boro, B.R. (2004), Profitability Improvement in the Refinery: A Case Study of the Bongaigaon Refinery and Petrochemicals, Master's Thesis, University of Ljubljana, Slovenia.

Coelli, T. (1996), *A Guide to FRONTIER Version 4.1*, CEPA, Univ. of New England, Armidale.

Coelli, T., Rao, D.S., and Battese, G. E. (1998), *An Introduction to Efficiency and Productivity Analysis*, Kluwer Academic Publishers, London.

Cornwell, C., P. Schmidt and R.C. Sickles (1990), Production Frontiers With Cross-sectional and Time-series Variation in Efficiency levels, *Journal of Econometrics*, 46, 185-200.

Datta, M (2006), Measurement of Capital Stock: the PIM and the Equivalent Proportional Depreciation Approach, *Indian Economic Review*, 41(2).

Datta, M. (2008), Reform and Technical Efficiency in Public Sector Oil Refining in India, *Journal of Quantitative Economics,* 6(1&2).

Felipe, J. and F.M. Fisher (2008), Aggregation (production), in Durlauf, S.N. and Blume, L.E. (eds), *The New Palgrave Dictionary of Economics*. Second Edition, Palgrave Macmillan.

Fisher, F. (1965), Embodied Technical Change and the Existence of an Aggregate Capital Stock, *Review of Economic Studies*, 32.

Foley, D.K. and Michl, T.R. (1999), *Growth and Distribution*, Harvard University Press, Cambridge, Massachusetts.

Gary, J.H. and G.E. Handwerk (2001), *Petroleum Refining: Technology and Economics*, Fourth Edition, Marcel Dekker, New York.

Government of India, Ministry of Petroleum and Natural Gas, *Executive Summary, Outcome Budget 2010-11*, Refineries in India, website.

Government of India (2009 and 2010), *Petroleum and Natural Gas Statistics*, MoPNG, N. Delhi.

Govvernment of India (2009), *Basic Statistics on Petroleum and Natural Gas*, MoPNG, N. Delhi.

Government of India (different years), *Public Enterprises Survey*, Department of Heavy Industries and Public Enterprises, N. Delhi.

Government of India (2010), *Report of the Expert Group on a Viable and Sustainable System of Pricing of Petroleum Products*, N. Delhi.

Greenwood, J. and B. Jovanovic (2001), Accounting for Growth, in Hulten, C.R. *et.al., New Developments in Productivity Analysis*, University of Chicago Press, Chicago.

Griliches, Z. (1992), Introduction to *Output Measurement in the Service Sector*, The University of Chicago Press, Chicago.

Griliches, Z. (1994), Productivity, R&D and the Data Constraint, *American Economic Review,* 84(1), Quoted from Berndt, E.R. and C.R. Hulten, 2007, *Hard to Measure Goods and Services: Essays in Honour of Zvi Griliches*, The University of Chicago Press, Chicago.

Griliches, Z. (1996), Discovery of the Residual, *Journal of Economic Literature*, 34(3), September.

Heravi, S. and Silver, M. (2007), Different Approaches to Estimating Hedonic Indexes, in *Hard-to-Measure Goods and Services*, eds., E.R. Berndt and C. R. Hulten, Essays in Honor of Zvi Griliches, University of Chicago Press, Chicago.

Hulten, C.R. (2001), Total Factor Productivity: A Short Biography, in Hulten, C.R. *et.al., New Developments in Productivity Analysis*, University of Chicago Press, Chicago.

Jondrow, J., Lovell, C.A.K, Materov, I.S. and, Schmidt, P. (1982), On Estimation of Technical Efficiency in the Stochastic Production Frontier Models, *Journal of Econometrics*, 19, 233-238.

Kodde, D.A., and Palm, F.C. (1986), Wald Criteria for Jointly Testing Equality and Inequality Restrictions, *Econometrica*, 54, 1243-48.

Kumbhakar, S., and Lovell, C.A.K. (2000), *Stochastic Frontier Analysis*, CUP., Cambridge, U.K.

Leibenstein, H. (1966), Allocative Efficiency *vs.* X-Efficiency, *American Economic Review*, 56(3), pp. 392-415.

Maples, R.E. (2000), *Petroleum Refinery Process Economics* (2nd Edition), Penn Well Corporation, Oklahoma.

Meeusen, W. and J. van den Broeck (1977), Efficiency Estimation from Cobb-Douglas Production Functions with Composed Error, *Internationsl Eocnomic Review*, 18(2), June, 435-44.

Nadiri, M.I. (1970), Some Approaches to the Theory and Measurement of Total Factor Productivity: A Survey, *Journal of Economic Literature*, 8(4), December.

Neogi, C. and Ghosh, B. (1994), Intertemporal Efficiency Variations in Indian Manufacturing Industries, *Journal of Productivity Analysis*, 5(3).

Page, J.M. (Jr.) (1984), Firm Size and Technical Efficiency: Application of Production Frontiers to Indian Survey Data, *Journal of Development Economics*, 16, 129-152.

Ray, S.C. (2004), *Data Development Analysis: Theory and Techniques for Economics and Operations Research*, Cambridge, U.K.

Schmidt, P. and Sickles, R.C. (1984), Production Frontiers and Panel Data, *Journal of Business and Economic Statistics*, 2, 367-74.

Sen, A.K. (1983), Carrots, Sticks and Economics: Perception Problems in Incentives, *Indian Economic review*, XVIII (1).

Solow, R.M. (2001), After "Technical Progress and the Aggregate Production Function", in Hulten, C.R., E.R. Dean and M.J. Harper., *New Developments in Productivity Analysis*, University of Chicago Press, Chicago.

Stevenson, R.E. (1980), Likelihood Functions for Generalized Stochastic Frontier Estimation, *Journal of Econometrics*, 13 (1), 57-66.

Stigler, (1976), The Xistence of X-Efficiency, American *Economic Review*, American *Economic* Association, vol. 66(1).

Stofan, E.R., *et al.* (2007), Lakes of Titan, *Nature*, 445, 61-64, 4 January.

Taylor, J. (1806), The Star in Rhymes for the Nursery by Ann and Jane Taylor, London, quoted in I. Opie and P. Opie, *The Oxford Dictionary of Nursery Rhymes*, Oxford University Press, 1951, 2nd edn., 1997.

Tsvetkov, L.A. (1985), *Organic Chemistry*, Mir Publisher, Moscow.

US Energy Information Administration (2004), *International Energy Annual.*